Christmas 1995

Hope you enjoy this trip into nostalgia.

BROTHER JIM

and Maryfrew

Palisades Amusement Park

A Century of Fond Memories

Palisades Amusement Park

A Century of Fond Memories

VINCE GARGIULO

Contributing Editors:
Edward Malillo and
Richard H. Haufe

Original Illustrations
by Edward Mascala

Rutgers University Press

New Brunswick, New Jersey

Library of Congress Cataloging-in-Publication Data

Gargiulo, Vince

Palisades Amusement Park: a century of fond memories / Vince Gargiulo

p.   cm.

Includes bibliographical references (p.) and index.

ISBN 0-8135-2224-2

1. Palisades Amusement Park (N.J.)—History.

I. Title.

GV1853.3.N52P354   1995

791' .06'874921—dc20   95-14484

Published by Rutgers University Press,
New Brunswick, New Jersey

Manufactured in the United
States of America

For everyone who knew Palisades . . .

everyone who ever loved an amusement park . . .

and everyone who is young at heart

Contents

Foreword
Cousin Bruce Morrow

To refer to Palisades Amusement Park as merely an "amusement park" is like calling Artur Rubinstein a piano player or like calling a bagel a slice of toasted white bread. "Palisades" (as we always called it) is (notice how I refer to it in the present tense) an integral part of our lives. Anybody who has played, visited, or been touched by this magical kingdom retains the glow from a very special relationship. For this place was like going home; visiting a close relative and enjoying the pleasure of a safe, relaxing, informal adventure; and, most important, sharing that wonderful feeling of freedom.

What was it about Palisades that gave it that safe family feeling? It was one thing, actually, one man, Uncle Irving, Irving Rosenthal— a five-foot, two-inch giant—the last of the old-time showmen. This breed of person had to be brought up in a different time, a different generation. These energetic, strong individuals were old-fashioned in the true sense of the word. They were go-getters, get-out-of-my-way-I'm-coming-through Americans, with the belief that nothing was impossible. I have just painted the perfect portrait of Uncle Irving, a renaissance man built to last and outlast everybody. Irving Rosenthal was the engineer and absolute spirit of that emotion called Palisades. Oh, yes, there were several talented people that contributed to the success of Palisades, but honestly, we were all his helpers and messengers. Let it be officially known to all good men and women present that Uncle Irving was the main ingredient to the Park's success and staying power.

My brief (a decade) tenure at Palisades proved to be not only a turning point in my career, but also an important schoolroom experience for me. It was here that I learned about the closeness of my audience. I developed long-lasting friendships with the stars of my shows and with the fans who are with me to this day. Palisades set the stage for music, but more important, helped us all to grow up a little. Those weekends together taught us to share with and respect other people. The physical design of the park forced us to recognize life around us. There were those occasions when individuals would not join the crowd and share that special feeling. They were quickly asked to leave (usually by Uncle Irving). Those now-legendary stage shows, watching our musical heroes lip syncing their songs while sitting under a warm sun and smelling popcorn, cotton candy, and those unforgettable french fries with vinegar, are indelibly etched in all of our souls. We shared each other at Palisades Amusement Park. It was a time of innocence, a time of growing, and, especially, a Happy Time.

I would like to propose to my friends of Cliffside Park and Fort Lee, New Jersey, that a small monument be erected at the area that was the main entrance to the park. I would like to have a likeness of Uncle Irving Rosenthal on the plaque and a few words like: "Here we were happy, here we grew! This is dedicated to the men and women who worked and played at Palisades Amusement Park, especially to the man who was and is its Spirit, its Shaker and its Mover—Irving Rosenthal." I will always cherish my memories.

From the Author

As I conducted my years of research into Palisades Amusement Park, I was often asked why I had such a devotion to an amusement park that had closed more than twenty years ago. Few people who grew up in and around Bergen County, New Jersey, ever needed to ask that question. They knew the answer. There was a very special magic to Palisades: it was *our* Park, *our* playground, *our* backyard. Few of us ever thought the Park wouldn't be there. It was our home, and no one could take away our home.

I grew up in Cliffside Park when Palisades was in its heyday. Our house was about fifteen blocks from the amusement park, yet on a quiet summer afternoon I could lean out my bedroom window and hear the screams of the riders as the roller coaster train took its first heart-pounding plunge. From the stages of Palisades, radio station disk jockeys introduced Diana Ross, Tony Bennett, Frankie Avalon, Smokey Warren, The Jackson Five, Bobby Rydell, and countless others. (The top deejay of his day, Cousin Bruce Morrow, became a household word thanks, in part, to his weekly appearances at Palisades.)

I, like many others, ignored the rumors of the Park's closing, until in 1971 the rumors became true. Yet years after the Park was leveled, people would still talk about the dips of the Cyclone coaster,

Photo: Victor Caratenuto

the vinegar-soaked french fries, Cousin Brucie's Top 40 shows, the colorful rides, and the cacophony of sounds on the midways.

Feeling nostalgic for a place that had been so much a part of my growing up, I began to research its history. I was amazed to discover its age and its origins. Born at the turn of the century, Palisades projected the whimsical side of our national character. Hand-built of wood, metal, grease, and the sweat of colorful individuals, it had a personality of its own and a long, enchanting history.

I became fascinated by its connections to Hollywood during the 1920s, when celebrities such as W. C. Fields, Jean Harlow, Johnny Weismuller, and Jackie Coogan could be found lounging around the Park's swimming pool. I found that much of its story parallels the history of America in the twentieth century. As the nation changed shape, so did the Park. Rides and attractions reflected the current events of the day. When Americans became fascinated with airships, the Park took to the skies with dirigibles. When the nation went to war, the Park's rides took on a patriotic theme. When our goal was placing a man on the moon, several rides had outer space themes, such as Apollo 14 or Trip to the Moon.

People fell in love with Palisades Amusement Park and *at* Palisades Amusement Park, where the Tunnel of Love originated and couples were married on the carousel and roller coaster. (In fact, ride operators often played matchmaker by pairing together single men and women.) Today, of course, a new generation of outdoor entertainment centers is taking over: corporate-owned, computer-designed theme parks, built of tubular steel and plastic. But Palisades was a magical place filled with love, happiness, and memories . . . almost a century of fond memories. There will never be another place like it.

Vince Gargiulo
March 1995

Acknowledgments

I am indebted to so many people who helped in the completion of this book. I would like to thank Ed Mascala for the beautiful artwork. Thanks also to Richard Haufe for his countless hours of research in the library. To America's favorite cousin, Bruce Morrow, goes my gratitude for helping me sort the facts from the fiction.

My very special appreciation goes to Amy Manndel for her unwavering support and the patience she displayed during the creation of this work.

Special thanks must be extended to Morgan "Mickey" Hughes, Bob Nesoff, Sol Abrams, John Rinaldi, and John Winkler for each of their contributions. Others who have contributed their time, wisdom, photos, or reminiscences to the completion of this book include:

Lois Adzima
Charlie Allen
Terri Auchard and *The Record*
Lou Azzollini
Tony Belmont (Alan Freed Productions)
Frank Berado
Malcolm Borg and *The Record*
Jack Bozzuffi
Phil Brooks

Liz Brown
Eileen Brunelli
Mayor Gerald Calabrese
Freddy "Boom Boom" Cannon
Mary Carpino
Edward and Jan Cavallo
Frank Cavallo
Steve Cavallo and The Palisades Park Library
Cathy Clark

Steve Clayton
Cliffside Park Mayor and Council
The staff of the Cliffside Park Public Library
Jackie Cooper
Eileen Copriski
Glenn Corbett
Nick Corbiscello
John Corrado
Mary Helen Corrado
Joe Costantino
Bill Courtney
Joe Criscione
Rich Criscione
Angelo D'Arminio
Clem Daniele
Sally Deering and *Gold Coast Magazine*
Maria DeVeyga, Edgewater Residential

Jerry Digney (Larry Harmon Pictures)
Bill Domiano
Edward Doublier
Patricia Durkin
Tim Egan
Sonny Fox
Herbert Frankel
Norman Frankel
Jane Galgoci
Roxanne Gambino
Bob "Statman" Gargiulo
Jerry and Joan Gargiulo
Jim Gargiulo
Vincent Gargiulo, Sr.
Randy Geisler
Sam Gnasso
John Graff
Richard Green
Tom Grissom
Eddie Guerra

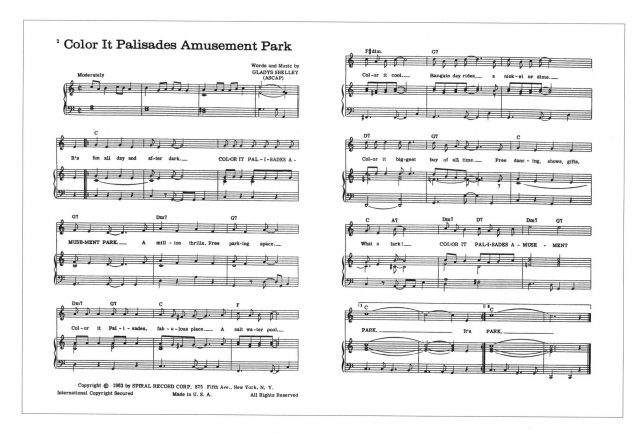

Palisades Amusement Park

Dianne Gutscher

Buddy Hackett

Douglas Hall

Michael and Diane
    Handschin

Rich Hanley

Tom Hanlon

Al Heget

Patti Hogan

Dave Hoolehan

Gertrude Hopler

Steve Howard

Ann Hughes and Kennywood
    Amusement Park

Anthony Isnardi

Steve Kelleher

Lucille Kelley

Thomas Knapp

Peter Kruimer

Joan and Pier Lagasi

Mary Lauro

Thomas Leahy

Richard Lebrone

Brad Levine

Jan LeWinter

Tony Litrenta

Marie Lopian

Maie McAskill

Dona McDermott

Brian McGuirt

Aseneath McKee

J. McKenna

Roseanne Maione

Tony Maione

Julie Ann Mairs

Ed Malillo

Jay Mallikoff

William A. Manning and *Fire
    Engineering Magazine*

Ann Mazzone

Memories Restaurant

Tom Meyers

J. Mioduszewski

Anna Morrone

Freddie Morrone

Joe Moscata

Mary Mulroy

John Nagy

National Archives, Washington,
    D.C.

New York City Police Anchor
    Club

Peter Noto

Carolyn Oberndorf

Kathy O'Connell

Thomas O'Donnell

Elizabeth O'Keefe

Pat Pallotta

Jack Palmer

Michael Peragine

William Pfeuffer

Peter Prinz

Tony Prisco

PSE&G Library

Andrew Ranaudo

Corrine Rinaldi

John Rinaldi, Jr.

Fred Roberge

Bruce Roberts

Nicki Rogers

John Rokeach

Tommy Romano

Anee Rossi

Robert J. Sapanara and *The
    Record*

Richie Schiess

Winnie Schneibener

Jack Schneider

Dian Scott

Sandy Shaffer

Gladys Shelley

P. J. Shelley

Trevor Sherwood

Bill Singer

Jimmy Sturr

E. Michael Sweeney

Acknowledgments

•

Noreene Sweeney
Miriam Taub
Jill Thomson
Teddy Venedis
Ruth Von Wagoner
Smokey Warren
Larry Wehrhahn
Judy Whitworth
George Wilson
Bob Wineshaw

Margaret Winkler
John Wolfe
Mark Wyatt and *Inside Track Magazine*
Margaret Wylie
Rich Youmans
Jacklyn Zeman
Harry Zerrenner
Janine Zucchet

They have all helped in their own way, and to all of them I say, "Thank you one and all."

The Early Years

1898-1909

AMERICAN workers were at a turning point during the late 1800s, when almost two million people belonged to organized labor unions that fought for better wages and shorter working hours. By the 1890s, though most Americans still worked six days a week, several unions had finally achieved the eight-hour workday. Workers were now able to enjoy something previously scarce: leisure time.

The chief mode of transit during this period was the trolley, which primarily carried people to and from their jobs every day. With more time after work for routine chores during the week, people were now able to spend their one day off with their families—and the trolley companies soon saw a way to use this to their advantage. Since power companies charged the lines a flat monthly fee for electricity whether the trolleys were busy or not, the six-day workweek meant little or no profit on Sundays. The companies needed some other means to encourage ridership on this day, so they decided to establish attractions that would lure families with the promise of recreation and relaxation. Those lines lucky enough to have beaches or lakes along their routes promoted them for family outings. Companies without these natural fun spots created their own attractions—band shells, picnic groves, and dance halls—to lure riders. These amusement areas became the groundwork for the traditional American amusement park. They were known as trolley parks, simple groves adorned with beautiful gardens, swings, refreshment stands, and gazebos. Families could pack a picnic lunch, board the

Above, left. The Horseshoe Curve ascending the cliffs of the Palisades. (Edgewater Free Public Library)

Above, right. Trolley tracks wind 200 feet up the cliffs (*The Palisadian*)

Right. The Bergen County Traction Company trolley car (Edgewater Free Public Library)

trolley, and enjoy a day out for very little cost. By locating the parks at the end of the line, the trolley companies ensured that patrons wouldn't be able to walk to them.

In the mid-1890s, the Bergen County Traction Company in New Jersey purchased thirty-eight acres of undeveloped, wooded land in the communities of Cliffside Park and Fort Lee. These two towns, located less than a mile from the burgeoning metropolis of New York City, lay two hundred feet above the Hudson River on columnar cliffs that resembled the walls of a fort—and seemed just as formidable. For most of the nineteenth century these cliffs—or Palisades, as they came to be called—had kept the area from the waves of progress that were washing over the rest of the United States. As a result, Fort Lee and Cliffside Park consisted mainly of tiny cottages, lush green farmland, and dense forest. It wasn't until 1896, as the growth of New York City spilled across the Hudson, that an electric railway was constructed to zigzag its way up the cliffs, making a sharp turn at what became known as the Horseshoe Curve.

The trolley company's newly purchased land boasted tall,

Top. The Hudson River ferry boat (Palisades Amusement Park Historical Society)

Above, left. From the Palisades, Grant's Tomb was clearly visible. (*The Palisadian*)

Above, right. The Gazebo—one of the first attractions of the Park (Cliffside Park Free Public Library)

stately oaks and large, rugged rocks that dotted the landscape, and it offered a magnificent view of New York City. Flower gardens were planted, picnic groves were established, and a walkway was laid to take advantage of the unforgettable view across the Hudson. This land was opened to the public in 1898 and christened the Park on the Palisades.

Lights, Camera, Palisades

By 1906, the wilderness of New Jersey had become a veritable oasis for early filmmakers eager to find new and interesting locations for their early flickers, as they were called. Although New York was a natural center for filmmaking, northern New Jersey offered a diverse terrain—from the cliffs of the Palisades to the burgeoning towns in Bergen County to the stark wilderness of the Delaware Water Gap—within a relatively short distance of New York City.

The Great Train Robbery, Thomas Edison's first full-length feature, was filmed near rural Paterson. Farther east, the dense forests of towns such as Fort Lee provided rustic backdrops for photo plays like *The Barnstormers* and *The Lone Highwayman*, both filmed at the Park on the Palisades. Edwin S. Porter, producer of *The Great Train Robbery*, also used the Palisades to film a movie titled *Rescued from an Eagle's Nest*.

With unimagined success, the motion picture industry in Fort Lee grew. Film studios sprang up like mushrooms: the Goldwyn Company, Victor Film Company, Kalem Studios, Triangle Studios, Universal Studios. Buildings resembling ramshackle airplane hangars emerged along the main streets of Fort Lee. The sleepy little community would never be the same.

Filmdom's newest star, Pearl White, heroine of the *Perils of Pauline*, spent most of her screen time dangling over the murky depths of the Hudson, two hundred feet below. Indeed, the catch phrase "cliffhanger" was coined on the Fort Lee Palisades.

Below, left. Early New Jersey movie makers (Cliffside Park Free Public Library)

Below, right. Pearl White filming on the cliffs of the Palisades (Tom Hanlon)

★ ★

For nearly a decade, the Park on the Palisades flourished and prospered. When ridership was down, the trolley line simply added new features; another gazebo, new decorative shrubbery, extra picnic tables, or perhaps some exotic flower gardens.

In December 1907, a syndicate of anonymous investors paid a reported $400,000 for the property. The new owners then announced plans to divide the property into twenty-four individual lots and build cheap cold-water flats. The uproar was tumultuous.

In the local newspaper, the *Palisadian*, one citizen declared, "The Park is so essentially a belonging of the public that to take it away now would be the direst calamity."

Another said, "I don't believe they would dare put up cheap tenements in the Park. I cannot believe we are to see this beautiful Park so despoiled."

Still another resident said, "Millions every year travel far greater distances in New York to get the breath of Central Park. Can there be a greater argument in favor of preserving the Park on the Palisades?"

One voice almost literally crying in the wilderness was that of an Episcopal minister from the nearby town of Edgewater, Reverend Dr. McCleary: "Here is nature in all its sublime simplicity. Who can enter such a place without the thought springing from the heart and mind? God is here, and he is my God."

Even the famous J. Pierpont Morgan threw his hat in the ring, with an endowment of $125,000 for the preservation of the Palisades.

By the spring of 1908, a compromise had been reached between the owners and the residents. In May, local newspapers reported that the Kiralfys, a celebrated family of show people, had purchased the Park to build a resort similar to Coney Island's Dreamland and Luna Park.

At the time, Coney Island consisted of three individual amusement parks. The oldest of these was Steeplechase, built on fifteen acres by George Tilyou in 1897. The success of Steeplechase prompted a second park to be opened in 1903, the twenty-two-acre Luna Park, which immediately captured the imagination of the population. Patrons had never seen as many lights illuminating the night skies as Luna had to offer. The following year, Dreamland opened. Dreamland had as many lights as Luna, but even more lavish and ornate buildings and towers. Coney Island was becoming a national obsession.

In the communities surrounding Palisades, the consensus was that the Park should remain a picnic grove rather than become an

Above. An oasis for suburban dwellers (Author's collection)

Left. Lovers' Lane, Palisades Park (*The Palisadian*)

Above, left. August Neumann, the first mayor of Cliffside Park (*The Palisadian*)

Above, right. The original main entrance to the Park (Palisades Amusement Park Historical Society)

Left. Alven H. Dexter (*The Palisadian*)

amusement resort, but even an amusement resort was better than cheap cold-water flats.

But Bolossy Kiralfy, the head of the concern that was reported to have taken over the Park, denied the newspaper reports as rumor. As it turned out, the Park had been purchased from the Bergen County Traction Company by August Neumann and Frank Knox. A native of Germany, Neumann had become the first mayor of Cliffside Park in March 1895; he served continuously for twelve years before he retired to try out civilian life. Knox was a real-estate developer, widely known around the area, who had named a section of Cliffside Park "Grantwood" because of its location directly across the Hudson River from Grant's Tomb. Neumann and Knox acquired the Park but kept an extremely low profile. Their ownership was never made public.

For the 1908 season the two men hired Alven H. Dexter to manage the Park. Dexter was well known in theatrical circles in the east. Born in the suburbs of Boston, he designed and supervised the building of the Lincoln Square theater in New York, then served as its first manager and ran it successfully for several years. He also managed the Boston Grand Opera House and remodeled the old public library in that city. Dexter was to become the first in a line of outstanding showmen who guided Palisades to the top of the amusement industry.

With Dexter at the helm, the Park on the Palisades began to acquire the look that would become its trademark and make it famous: a balanced blend of entertainment, nature, and colorful attractions. Workers strung through the trees some fifteen thousand electric lights—"Edison's wonders"—which were still relatively new to the local residents. There were new chowder and hot dog stands, games of skill, and confectioneries that could remain open all night. In the opinion of some, it would be like living next to Fairyland.

"There is no place around New York so beautifully adapted for holding picnics, and the management offers special inducements to lodges, societies, associations, Sunday Schools, etc," read the policy statement made by Park management in 1908. These inducements would be accepted by many community groups throughout the Park's existence.

On opening night in May 1908, as many as three thousand people—nearly half of the area's population—came to behold this new curiosity and see the wondrous new attractions. A miniature train carried passengers around a one-thousand-foot track. Bonthron & Elkin's Riding Academy offered the chance to ride horseback down a five-hundred-foot bridal path. Patrons could also enjoy a ride on the swings or on the newly installed D. C. Miller & Co. carousel; the carousel riders could choose from a variety of ornately carved animals and, when in the mood, take a whirl at catching the brass rings. When they needed a break, customers could find soft drinks, cakes, ice cream, and a fine assortment of cigars and cigarettes at the Refreshment Pavilion.

A number of games and attractions were also introduced. These included:

- **Days of 49.** A game with a guaranteed winner in which the player threw darts at a board covered with numbers. The total number accumulated from all throws decided which prize a patron would receive.
- **The Disk Stein Board.** Billed as a game of "science and skill," this concession was run by Captain Jack Smith, who became known as the "champion revolver shot in the world" after winning a competition at Madison Square Garden in 1901. It offered fine imported steins (one of which was said to be valued at $100), vases, and china sets as prizes. Patrons threw six-inch brass disks onto a table covered with red numbered circles, which varied from five to eight inches in diameter. If a disk fell

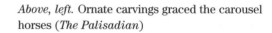

Above, left. Ornate carvings graced the carousel horses (*The Palisadian*)

Above, right. The beautiful carousel at Palisades (*The Palisadian*)

Left. Simple attractions, like these swings, drew people into the Park for weekend fun. (*The Palisadian*)

Below. The Refreshment Pavilion (*The Palisadian*)

Palisades Amusement Park

•

completely within any of the circles, that circle's number was matched to a corresponding prize.

- **Cane Board.** A game of skill in which the patron tossed small wooden rings at a variety of walking canes, the heads of which protruded through a stretched canvas. If the ring landed around one of the canes, the patron could take that cane home. Of course, the larger and more ornate the head, the more difficult it was to win.

- **Knife Board.** In this game, which was similar to the Cane Board, patrons won pocket knives by tossing rings at an angled board from which the knives extended.

- **Shooting Gallery.** Under the management of R. L. Cook, the nation's premier builder of shooting galleries, the Park's gallery offered moving targets and boasted the finest rifles and revolvers—including real Colts and Smith & Wessons.

- **The Apple Game.** Wooden rings were thrown over apples on a table, with each apple containing the number of a prize.

- **The World's Most Daring High Diver.** A former world-champion high diver, Arthur Holden first burst upon the world's stage on September 23, 1896, when he dove off the Brooklyn Bridge. Except for a two-year hiatus and a five-year world tour, Holden performed the high dive at the Park from 1908 until at least 1937, when he was sixty-nine years old. He awed crowds twice daily by diving backwards, from a platform 105 feet in the air, into a pool that measured just thirteen feet long, eight feet wide, and about five feet deep. It is believed that Holden accomplished his amazing dives with the aid of a tightly stretched net set up in the bottom of the pool. However it was done, this was not a feat to attempt at home: Holden suffered many injuries—including broken legs and ribs, a broken arm, and a broken foot—during his decades of entertaining Park crowds.

- **Carlisle and Robbins Wild West Show.** The natural beauty of the Park provided a ready-made backdrop for a show of this kind. The star of the show was Nebraska Bill, a tall, husky fellow from the state bearing his name. His troupe included a band of Indians, a dozen cowboys, dashing lady riders, a drove of ponies, bucking broncos, and his own trick horse. Its acts earned the Wild West Show a commanding position on the grounds.

- **Captain Charles Oliver Jones and His Dirigible Balloon.** In 1904, the first American-built dirigible rose into the skies. Within a few years after that historic event, the Park hired Captain Charles Oliver Jones, the most famous aeronaut of his time,

Arthur Holden, high diver (*The Palisadian*)

Sketch of the Park showing the Carlisle and Robbins Wild West Show at the center (*The Palisadian*)

to make daily ascensions in his own cigar-shaped dirigible, *The Boomerang.* Propelled by a thirty-horsepower engine, *The Boomerang* measured 24 feet in diameter and 105 feet in length, and its balloon contained twenty-five thousand cubic feet of gas. The four-foot-square car had a wooden bench for the operator and, with careful squeezing, two passengers (although patrons were not permitted to ride in the aircraft).

- **Daily Balloon Flights across the Hudson.** Though balloon shows were not new to turn-of-the-century audiences, the Park used its location on the Palisades to showcase daily flights to New York's Battery Park or Washington Heights. Of course, problems occasionally occurred. Changing winds along the Hudson would result in unplanned descents onto the shore of Long Island Sound or into the river itself. The planned ascent for August 29, 1909, had to be canceled when a balloon was held for ransom; an irate member of the Edgewater Motor Boat Club demanded $100 for damages incurred when the balloon crash-landed on his craft in the middle of the river. (After deliberating

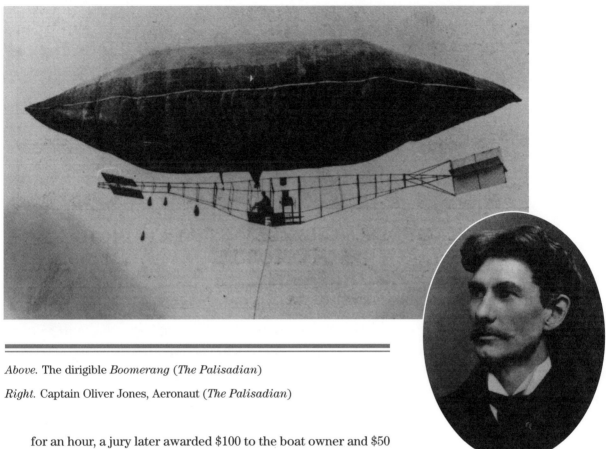

Above. The dirigible *Boomerang* (*The Palisadian*)

Right. Captain Oliver Jones, Aeronaut (*The Palisadian*)

for an hour, a jury later awarded $100 to the boat owner and $50 to the balloon owner for having been deprived of the use of his air bag.)

- **Lady Beneta.** This young lady balloonist, who thrilled crowds when she ascended over the Park and then parachuted onto the grounds, also shocked the public by her scant attire, which she wore while taking the trolley to and from work or while riding the streets on her bicycle. Local residents cried for the management to furnish her with a bathrobe.

- **The Dancing Pavilion.** This handsome building was two hundred feet long by fifty feet wide, with kitchen and lavatories in a seventy-five-foot rear extension. The dance floor, made of polished hardwood, measured about 120 feet long. The pavilion sparked a great deal of controversy in the surrounding community as dancing on Sunday was considered a violation of God's law. As one local newspaper said, "This is all right for those who go there for that purpose and who do not regard the Sabbath as any better than any other day, but the moral sentiment of the

The Early Years, 1898–1909

community is against dancing on Sunday. The public will patronize the Park Sunday without these objectionable features."

- **Professor R. J. Blake's Hippodrome Circus.** At the north end of the midway, in a special blue-and-white–striped tent, Professor Blake presented his dog, pony, and monkey circus. Professor Blake appeared in vaudeville all winter following the summer shows, and he was also well known at Coney Island. Children loved this special show at the Park and especially the comedy antics of Maud, the famous bucking mule, who resisted all efforts at being ridden.
- **Open-Air Theatre.** This outdoor amphitheatre offered the finest stage performers and vaudeville acts of the era. The breezes blowing up from the Hudson River provided cool relief on hot summer days, as did the shade from leafy branches of surrounding trees.
- **High-Diving Horses.** In 1905, Atlantic City's Steel Pier had introduced a high-diving horse act that made headlines. In an effort to keep up with the competition, Palisades brought in the celebrated Gorman horses, a novelty act that featured two beautiful steeds, "King" and "Queen," who took turns performing for the crowds. Each horse carried a woman on its back as it leapt toward a tank of water forty feet below.

For the quiet little towns of Fort Lee and Cliffside Park, these attractions took some getting used to. Less than a month after the Park's opening that season, residents began to lodge complaints about the noise of the crowds that waited for the trolley each night. These grievances were just the beginning of many that would plague the Park throughout its lifetime.

That year marked a turning point for the Park. In June it became known as Palisades Amusement Park and in November Dexter promised even more extensive improvements for the 1909 season—including a skating rink on the spot where the balloon ascensions were made during the summer months.

The thrills of change also brought additional stress. In March 1909, Dexter came down with influenza and remained in convalescence for ten days. He then developed bronchial pneumonia, from which he never recovered. On March 22, at the age of fifty-seven, Alven H. Dexter died. By most reports, he had been considered a worthy entrepreneur and a lovable man. Local historians referred to him as the father of the Park on the Palisades.

The management for the 1909 season fell to Albert Tusch and Samuel J. Byrne. Tusch was a low-key administrator who handled

Above. Interior, the Dancing Pavilion, ca. 1909 (*The Record*)

Right. Ad for the new open-air Summer Theatre (*The Palisadian*)

Below. The Dancing Pavilion (*The Palisadian*)

The rustic entrance to Palisades Park (*The Palisadian*)

mostly paperwork. Byrne, however, loved the limelight. A friend of Dexter's, Byrne was an even more auspicious showman than his predecessor, and his credentials encompassed international entertainment capitals. He succeeded Barnum and Bailey as lessee of the Olympia in London, the largest amusement structure in Great Britain. In New York, he managed the historic Lenox Lyceum at Madison Avenue and 57th Street.

Byrne promised to bring in the best attractions for the 1909 season. Many of the strongest features of Atlantic City and Coney Island, such as the diving horses and the multitude of lights, had been duplicated at Palisades. Now the Open-Air Theatre presented more elaborate musical comedies as well as the best vaudeville acts, which were procured through the services of the William Morris Agency. Palisades showcased the talents of some of that era's most popular stars, including Mae Ward, the Rosedale Quartette, Smirl and Kessnes, and The Three Judges.

Palisades Amusement Park reopened that spring of 1909 amid

Above. The early midways of Palisades Park (*The Record*)

Right. Ad (circa 1909) from *The Palisadian* newspaper (*The Palisadian*)

great public accolades, as a reported thirty thousand people passed through the gates that opening weekend. More than $750,000 had been spent on renovations and new attractions. These included the $15,000 Dance Hall Casino (designed by Granville Dexter, son of the late Alven), the Zoological Gardens, an aviary, and a farm. An Old Plantation Show promised visitors a glimpse of the pre–Civil War South "befo' de wah" and featured "genuine colored people who will sing plantation melodies in their happiest fashion." At Williard's Temple of Music—an exact duplicate of the Temple of Music at Coney Island's Dreamland—music was produced from everyday objects such as lighted parlor lamps, alarm clocks, and the seats in the theater. A Punch and Judy show was added, as was a separate children's playground with swings, sandboxes, and a teeter board. The Hindu Theater featured mind-reading and magic. An old-fash-ioned county fair, scheduled to open in September, would bring a touch of rural life to the bustling suburban area. And for conces-sionaires, the Park was a gold mine. (One candy parlor, Mampes', became so popular that special messengers were dispatched regu-larly to deliver boxes of caramel corn and fudge-covered nuts to local residents.)

The Early Years, 1898–1909
•

Thrill seekers were not slighted, either. A figure-eight toboggan slide promised delights to thousands of early roller-coaster enthusiasts who loved climbs, dips, and plunges. (For the next sixty-two years, Palisades Park would be home to some of the world's greatest and most famous roller coasters, including the wooden classic, the Cyclone.) The Death Swing was another thrilling attraction. A young lady daredevil sat in an automobile that was hoisted onto a platform sixty feet above the ground. At the woman's command, the car began its descent down the steep incline. When it reached the bottom of the roadway, iron hooks suspended from an overhead bar caught the car and whirled it end over end. Centrifugal force kept the young woman in her seat.

Newspapers of the day claimed the great Ferris wheel, resplen-

Above, right. The Miniature Railway (*The Palisadian*)

Right. Patrons came from far and wide to the new amusement park. (*The Palisadian*)

Top, left. Figure 8 Toboggan Slide, side view (*The Palisadian*)

Above. The Toboggan Slide, entrance (*The Palisadian*)

Top, right. The Death Swing thrilled patrons at the Palisades. (John and Margaret Winkler)

dent in its array of lights, stood four hundred feet above the Hudson. Though it's unlikely this was an accurate measurement, it is certain that by the spring of 1909 Palisades Amusement Park was clearly visible from across the river. Its southerly stretch, facing the riverfront, became known as the Grand Esplanade, and on it the new proprietor erected what was called the largest electric sign in the world. Built by the Globe Electric Company of New York, the sign was four hundred feet long and fitted with ten thousand incandescent bulbs that spelled out, in letters eighteen feet high, the words

The Early Years, 1898–1909
•

★ ★

Matchmaking at Palisades

One of the first weddings performed at Palisades was held in June 1909. Jack Hammond, the champion rifle shooter at the Wild West Show, married Clara Tunney, a cashier at the Park, in a ceremony held in the Park's administration building.

The following month, countless newspapers heralded the announcement of another wedding. Chief Deep Sky of the Sioux Indians would marry twenty-one-year-old Adele Rowland.

Miss Rowland had met the Indian chief at Palisades Park while he was performing in the Wild West Show. After the performance he was introduced to her, and a week later they were engaged. Many Sioux were opposed to his marrying outside the tribe, but eventually the head of the Sioux nation gave his consent. The couple were to be wed on Thursday, July 29, at the New York Polo Grounds, during the annual Theatrical Field Day events. Each year, actors, actresses, athletes, and acrobats participated in an exhibition baseball game, track and field events, and fun and frolic for the benefit of the New York Home for Destitute Crippled Children. That Thursday, a reported ten thousand people paid to watch the games and see the wedding. At the last minute, however, Miss Rowland backed out. Dorothy Newell, an actress with the Motor Girl company, stepped in to fill the role as bride. Just as Chief Deep Sky and Miss Newell were about to be wed, the band of Indians from the Park rode across the field, scooped up the bride-to-be, and carried her away. By this point, it had become fairly obvious that this entire romance had been a clever publicity stunt concocted by the Park. The Theatrical Managers and Actors' Association of America raised over $12,000 that day for charity.

Dorothy Newell and her new "husband" (John and Margaret Winkler)

★ ★

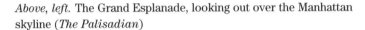

Above, left. The Grand Esplanade, looking out over the Manhattan skyline (*The Palisadian*)

Above, right. The Ferris Wheel (*The Palisadian*)

P-A-L-I-S-A-D-E-S A-M-U-S-E-M-E-N-T P-A-R-K. Press releases boasted that, on a dark night, the sign could be read from Babylon, Long Island, New York, about fifty miles away.

That year the Park also played host to the then largest outdoor meeting for the rights of women ever held in New York or New Jersey. Women's organizations from the two states assembled at the Park and gathered signatures for petitions seeking a constitutional amendment that would guarantee a woman's right to vote. Two booths were erected within the Park, one for New York and the other for New Jersey. The groups also sought to bring the temperate suffragists and their more militant sisters, the suffragettes, closer together. The entire Park was decorated in yellow, the suffragist color. Yellow badges adorned the lapels of patrons, thousands of golden flowers lined the Park, and yellow banners and streamers bedecked the walks and paths. Marchers carried banners up and down the midways. Renowned women in the movement such as Helen Murphy, chairwoman of the National Progressive Suffrage Union, and Sophie Loebinger, editor of the *American Suffragette*, delivered speeches. Even the Indian women from the Park's own Wild West Show demonstrated their support for women's rights. An estimated five thousand supporters, both men and women, attended the event, and thousands of signatures were added to the petitions.

The Early Years, 1898–1909

•

By the end of the twentieth century's first decade, Palisades Amusement Park had joined Coney Island and New York's Hippodrome as one of the country's premier attractions. The spirit of the times was captured in a song written by Nate Walker, manager of the Park's Monarch Moving Picture Show. A tribute to Walker's friend, the late Alven Dexter, the tune is titled "Take Me Up to Palisades Park":

Said Carrie to Larry,
"Now don't be contrary,
I'm not going down to the Isle;
It's too far to roam,
And I've got to get home,
I can only stay for a while;
We'll just take the ferry,
Go up in the airy,
High up on the old Palisade.
There's always a breeze
In the Park with the trees,
We'll roam thro' the woods in the shade."

CHORUS

Take me up, up, up,
High up to Palisades Park;
For up there we can spoon
By the light of the moon,
The best place I know for a lark;
Whirl me round, round, round,
Thro' a waltz or a two-step we'll glide;
With the cooing and wooing,
There's now something doing,
On the Jersey side.

The Hollywood Connection

1910-1935

*B*Y THE TIME the Park closed for the season on October 3, 1909, it had taken its position among America's favorite amusement resorts. The Park had enjoyed a highly successful season and had firmly established its character as clean and wholesome. The theater presented high-class bills, and alcohol and gambling were forbidden.

However, the cost of the Park's extensive renovations proved too great a burden for the owners to bear. In February 1910, the Park was purchased by the Palisades Realty and Amusement Company. This company was headed by Nicholas and Joseph Schenck, and its fiscal agent was the Realty Trust. The Schencks were the same gentlemen who in 1907 had been among the anonymous investors who attempted to build cold-water flats on the property. Now they had different plans.

Born in Rybinsk, Russia, the brothers came with their family to the United States in 1891; Joseph was thirteen and Nicholas was two years younger. For a time, the brothers earned money by selling newspapers. Then, at age twenty-one, Joseph landed a job working in a New York drugstore. He found work there for Nicholas as well, and within two years the enterprising brothers had purchased the store.

Several years later, while visiting Fort George Amusement Park on Third Avenue in New York City, the brothers recognized another potential source of profit. They opened a beer concession to serve the throngs of people who had to wait for the trolley to take them home. They also invested in a cane board and a knife board at Fort

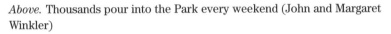

Above. Thousands pour into the Park every weekend (John and Margaret Winkler)

Above, right. Nicholas Schenck (John and Margaret Winkler)

Right. Joseph Schenck (John and Margaret Winkler)

George. Shrewd businessmen as they were, the Schencks also saw enormous potential in the entertainment industry, and they began providing vaudeville acts to the amusement park.

A steady customer at Fort George was a well-to-do entrepreneur named Marcus Loew. Loew had his roots in penny arcades and nickelodeon parlors, and he owned the Royal Theater in Brooklyn. He took a liking to the young Schenck brothers and loaned them enough money to establish several rides of their own in an area within Fort George Amusement Park. They named their new area Paradise Park.

Loew and the Schencks became partners in various business ventures, investing in theaters, nickelodeons, real estate, vaudeville acts, and motion pictures. In 1910 the Schencks wanted a larger showcase than Paradise Park could provide. So they turned their eyes across the Hudson, to the Park on the Palisades.

It had been their purpose, at first, to use the Park chiefly as a showcase for more of their nickelodeon parlors and penny arcades. However, it didn't take them long to realize that if people were eager to drop their hard-earned coins into a nickelodeon, they would pay even more for rides and games of skill.

The Hollywood Connection, 1910–1935

•

The Park—now officially known as the Schenck Brothers' Palisade Park, with the ornate front gate prominently displaying the name—quietly reopened in May 1910. Not everyone expressed happiness at this, however. After two short years, those who had welcomed the new Park as a magical Fairyland were now calling for its destruction. Even the clergy, those staunch, loyal Park defenders, were also rallying its demise, attacking it from a moral standpoint.

A band of vandals sawed and hacked down four huge billboards advertising the Park that were located along the Hudson River trolley tracks. Having succeeded in ridding their area of the unsightly billboards, two hundred residents from sections of Cliffside Park, Fort Lee, and Edgewater attempted to rid themselves of the Park. They converged on the new owners en masse and presented petitions. They cited the fact that more than half of the thousands who filed through the Park every week were from New York and its boroughs. The residents also bitterly opposed the "the screams of feminine passengers" riding the Switch Back coaster. (The Switch Back was only five hundred feet short of a mile in length, and the dips were thrillers.)

At a packed town council meeting, in the Palisades section of Fort Lee, local residents heatedly attacked the Park. One of the speakers at the meeting, Vincent B. Kelly, proclaimed, "From the comparatively harmless amusement park of two seasons ago, it has grown into an intolerable nuisance, a menace to the moral tone of three residential communities. The Park on the Palisades has been taken over by vandals who have transformed a beautiful, free public playground, fashioned by nature, into a cheap catchpenny imitation of the commonest features of Coney Island."

This would be a recurring theme in the complaints against the Park over the years. The Sunday Observance League joined the conflict, taking action against the Sunday opening of the Park. To make matters worse, the Schenck brothers seemed little concerned with the uproar. They were much too preoccupied with their new plans for the Park.

Over the next two years, the Schencks introduced several new features that greatly helped daily operations around the Park. They installed cement walks to define the midways, and directed grounds superintendent Fred Luff to plant thousands of floral displays recently transplanted from private hothouses. They established a baby nursery and employed trained nurses to care for the infants while their parents enjoyed the pleasures of the Park. (Claim checks were issued when the parents left their children, to avoid any confusion when it came time to pick up the little ones.) In 1911 they in-

Above. The walkways and gardens of the Park drew in the crowds. (*The Palisadian*)

Right. The new entrance of "Schenck Bros. Palisade Park" (Palisades Amusement Park Historical Society)

stalled at Palisades the first public address system, which consisted of forty-five separate stations that were dubbed "The Electric Enunciators." Any or all of the stations could be activated through a main switchboard located in the administration building. The announcer spoke into a funnel-shaped instrument, and his message was transmitted to the farthest ends of the grounds. Though this seems rather commonplace to today's public playgrounds, each Electric Enunciator became an attraction in itself.

The Park also featured a large searchlight on the cliffs of the

The Hollywood Connection, 1910–1935
•

Palisades. Every night, the light's operator moved the beam back and forth across the surface of the Hudson River. One evening in August 1911, members of a New York yacht club were looking out onto the river as the beam of light played on the water's surface. Suddenly, the beam illuminated three men tossing about in the middle of the river, an overturned boat floating nearby. Several members set off in their vessels while the searchlight operator kept the beacon of light fixed on the helpless trio. The three exhausted men were rescued and taken back to the club building for medical treatment. The event became so talked about that a motion picture company re-enacted the episode in a film called *Saved by Searchlight*.

The Schencks were also busy during this time acquiring new attractions for their patrons' enjoyment. These included:

- **The Automobile Race.** Many patrons had heard about this modern wonder called the automobile, but few owned one. This attraction, installed at the Park for the 1910 season, gave riders a chance to sit behind the wheel of a real car. Three automobiles were positioned at the top of a nineteen-hundred-foot incline. A barrier held the three vehicles in place until the race began. The cars reportedly reached speeds of up to sixty miles an hour. Various competitions were held and prizes were awarded to the victors.
- **The Sleigh Ride Coaster.** In this attraction, built near the main promenade in 1910, sled-like cars holding one or two people were hoisted sixty feet in the air, placed at the top of a large incline, then released to slide down four hundred feet. This ride, shaped to resemble a floe of icebergs, was perhaps the most picturesque in the Park.
- **Big Scenic Coaster.** Built in 1910 at a cost of $25,000, this coaster had four double cars, each seating six to seven people. The cars received their power from an electrified center rail, in much the same way a subway car receives power from a third rail. A motorman in the front seat piloted the coaster, which could go either forward or backward. The third rail drove the cars up the inclines, while gravity provided the source of power on the dips. (Although the dips looked dangerous, the management publicly assured riders of its safety.) The track ran for over forty-five hundred feet and the ride lasted 2½ to 3 minutes.

The Big Scenic was constructed near the front entrance, and from this location every screeching turn and shrill scream could be heard for miles around. This incited a series of complaints to

The Big Scenic Coaster (John and Margaret Winkler)

The Big Scenic Coaster (John and Margaret Winkler)

be lodged from residents about the noise. Once again, a cry went out to close the Park, and a lawsuit was filed. The case of the people versus the Schenck Brothers' Palisade Park was brought before Judge Cornelius Doremus of Hackensack. After much legal wrangling, the judge declared he had no intention of closing the Park. "To close up a resort representing such enormous vested interests would mean a stupendous undertaking," he said. After nearly a year, local residents and the Schencks finally reached a compromise. Since the main complaint seemed to emanate from the roller coaster, the Schencks agreed to close down the ride no later than ten o'clock every night.

- **The Aborn Opera Company.** Headed by Milton and Sargent Aborn, the firm had similar companies located in various cities across the United States. It began staging performances at the Park's Open-Air Theatre in 1911. Artists and productions were exchanged with each other in the same manner as that of the

The Hollywood Connection, 1910–1935
•

Above. Frank Goodale, boy aeronaut (John and Margaret Winkler)

Above, left. Goodale flies over New York City (John and Margaret Winkler)

Right. The Frolic ride thrilled patrons. (John and Margaret Winkler)

English Grand Opera Company. Sentimental immigrants became reacquainted with many of their favorite shows, including *Robin Hood*, Victor Herbert's *The Red Mill*, and George M. Cohan's *Little Johnny Jones*.

- **The French Hatching Cat.** This Angora feline had an affinity for sitting on eggs and being surrounded by baby chicks. In June

1911 Nick Schenck outbid other American amusement park owners for the right to display the famous kitty and booked it for a six-week stint.

- **The Great Lights Contest.** The question had been asked countless times; How many lights are there in Palisades Amusement Park? The Schencks decided to capitalize on the popular query by running a contest in June 1911. The man or woman who guessed closest to the exact number would win a gold watch. Contestants were free to count every bulb in the Park if they wished, but were warned that it took the Park's chief electrician and his assistants one whole week to get a total figure.

- **"The World's Youngest Boy Aeronaut."** When the Schencks took over at Palisades, they continued the tradition of dirigible air flights by hiring the Strobel International Aviation Company of Toledo, Ohio. The company supplied the Park with "the world's youngest boy aeronaut," Frank Goodale, who started his aerial career in 1907 at the age of eighteen. In 1911 the Schenck brothers decided to eliminate the middleman; they bought young Frank his own balloon and placed him on the Park's payroll. In May the airship company obtained an injunction prohibiting the young pilot from flying, claiming breach of contract; Goodale had three years remaining on his five-year pact with Strobel. After months of legal battle, the matter was settled out of court just in time for the young daredevil to be back in the skies for the July 4 holiday.

Another dispute made headlines in July 1911 when 125 cashiers at Palisades demanded their booths be equipped with modern conveniences such as hair brushes, combs, powder puffs, and mirrors. They also asked, if possible, for hot and cold running water in each booth.

A spokeswoman for the cashiers said, "We are confined all day in those narrow booths under the constant gaze of the crowds, with only an occasional chance to slip away and refreshen ourselves up a bit when the relief girls come around." When asked about the running water demands, she admitted, "We don't really expect to have hot and cold running water in each booth. We just stuck that demand in with the others so that when it comes time to compromise with Mr. Schenck, we can concede that point, thus showing how liberal-minded we are."

Nicholas Schenck told a reporter for the *New York Review* that the requests of the ladies were being considered.

DESPITE the occasional disputes, the Schencks enjoyed huge profits during their first three years of ownership. In 1913 they used those profits to turn a protracted dream into reality. Until then, their largest competitor had been Coney Island. Though the Brooklyn resort had its share of rides and attractions, much of its allure lay in its beaches. The Schencks decided they would have the same thing, and if they could not bring the Park to the beach, they would bring the beach to the Park!

The Schencks began to construct what would be billed as the largest outdoor saltwater pool in the world. Occupying the spacious property where Nebraska Bill had conducted his Wild West Show, it would be as wide as a city block and three times as long, with an island at its center on which swimmers could recline.

But the Schencks wanted more than just the world's largest pool. The brothers hired William F. Mangels, a well-known inventor who five years earlier had patented the system that gave carousel horses their galloping movement, and they directed him to design and install a wave-making machine for their novel swimming pool. To complete the illusion, several hundred tons of ocean sand were hauled from the Atlantic coastline to create an artificial beach. (In years to come, patrons would lose assorted valuables there just as they would on a real beach. In 1929, when Park workers prepared to replace the three feet of old sand, they found five necklaces, seven cigarette cases, eight cigarette holders, six pairs of beach glasses, four rings [including one with a diamond], four combs, a set of false teeth, a five-dollar gold piece, and approximately $25 in assorted bills and change.)

The one and a half million gallons of saltwater needed for the pool were siphoned from the Hudson River at high tide by enormous pumps. Before entering the pool, the water flowed through six large filters to clear it of any contaminants.

On June 8, 1913, the large pool officially opened at Palisades Park. Billed as being able to accommodate ten thousand swimmers, the pool was constructed entirely of concrete. Its depth ranged from a few inches to fourteen feet; at the deepest end, diving boards built from hickory timbers lined the sides. Bathhouses were divided equally among the sexes and provided accommodations for more than two thousand bathers. The Park even offered free swimming instructions to all patrons.

Every night at eleven o'clock the entire pool was drained, a process that took an average of five hours to complete. Six barrels of lime were used to thoroughly clean the bottom and all the walls. The pool was then refilled in plenty of time for the early morning bathers.

Above. The new swimming pool (The Corbett Collection)

Right. The Big Scenic Coaster (John and Margaret Winkler)

Below. The Open-Air Theatre (*The Palisadian*)

By the middle of the decade, the annual school picnic had become a tradition that would continue through the life of the Park. It marked the end of the school year and the beginning of summer, and it did so with style. The mayor, members of the town council and the board of education, and the chief of police (or their representatives) would lead a parade through Cliffside Park. As the procession passed each school, the students joined in the line of marchers. (The picnic was considered a part of the school's curriculum, and pupils and teachers were required to attend.) About two thousand schoolchildren, barely controlled and bolstered by the school band, advanced on the Park. There, after listening to a last plea for self-control, they burst through the gates and enveloped the grounds. For the rest of the day, they put school out of their minds and concentrated on sampling the delights of the Park, which after 1915 included the first public astronomical observatory in the United States. Three large telescopes allowed the students to scan the heavens—or spy on people walking the streets of Manhattan.

Another tradition was the Wednesday evening fireworks displays, which had begun in 1909. In 1915 the pyrotechnics exhibitions were expanded to every Tuesday and Thursday evenings. These thrilling displays would continue at the Park through the 1940s—and provide another source of complaint for local residents.

While the Great War raged in Europe, the Park continued to attract its patrons. In the spirit of the times, it offered attractions such as Bombardment, a spectacle that displayed battleships and submarines with startling realism, and Through the Dardanelles, a reproduction of the conflict over these Turkish straits. It displayed the location of the forts and the position of the battleships, which had been bombarding the mountainside towns.

By this time, Joseph Schenck had very little to do with the daily grind of running the amusement park. He had become consumed with the young motion picture business. Hollywood—or Hollywoodland, as it was originally known—had become the mecca of the entertainment industry, catering to an enormous American appetite for motion pictures.

In 1917, Joseph married silent film star Norma Talmadge. Though the marriage eventually failed—the couple would divorce in 1934—it helped bring the older Schenck brother to the attention of Lewis J. Selznick, father of David O. The elder Selznick invited Joseph to join his film operations; Joseph accepted and, for all intents and purposes, abandoned Palisades Park. Before the end of the decade, he was elected board chairman of the newly

★ ★

Miles of Merry Midway

In July 1915, an observer at Palisades Amusement Park noted there were "Miles of Merry Midway where every whirly-gig known to the out-of-door amusement promoter is in operation. There is not a dull moment in the street of amusement, as it is always alive with a merry laughing throng, who are fairly teeming with a holiday spirit."

That description conjures visions of exciting times on streets stretching to the horizon. Indeed, they seemed to do so. One could look down a midway, through the Park, and beyond to the skyline of New York City across the river. But just what is a midway?

The term originated at the 1893 Columbian Exposition in Chicago. The exposition's organizers decided to concentrate all of the amusements in one area. They chose a wide boulevard constructed twenty years earlier and aptly named Midway Plaisance ("plaisance" is French for pleasure.) Although millions did indeed have a pleasurable time, the area soon became known simply as the midway. Here George Washington Ferris showcased his Observation Wheel, today known by its builder's name. Friends met on the midway to ride the rides, play the games, and see the sights. Soon the term *midway* became widely used to mean any area that had amusements, concessions, games, and so on—a definition that encompassed the entire amusement park or carnival.

Today, it is generally accepted that *midway* refers to any avenue on which people stroll as they move from one grand attraction to another. The midways connect major pavilions or rides in the same manner as the shops of a mall connect the larger department stores. The classic midway-scape consists of smaller rides, games of chance, shooting galleries, palm readers, souvenir stands, barkers, lights, crowds, and excitement. From its numerous food stands, the mouth-watering smells of cotton candy, Belgian waffles, hamburgers, hot dogs, and giant pretzels float and mingle up and down its paths. If the rides are the heart of an amusement park, then the midways compose the skeleton that holds the park together.

★ ★

formed United Artists Corporation, which had been established by D.W. Griffith, Mary Pickford, Charlie Chaplin, and Douglas Fairbanks.

Joseph wasn't the only Schenck brother lured by the magic of motion pictures. Though the movie-making industry was a cutthroat business in which partners would sell out partners without hesitation, the Schencks had kept a tight alliance with Loew—largely because Loew, a theater-owner extraordinaire, controlled the purse strings. In 1919 Nicholas Schenck was made president and general manager of Loews, Inc.

To safeguard their profitable interests, Loew and the Schencks continued to buy up not only theaters, but movie studios as well. In 1924, to keep his theaters supplied with a steady flow of pictures, Marcus Loew effected the merger of Metro Pictures Corporation, the Goldwyn Studios, and Louis B. Mayer Productions into a single

The Hollywood Connection, 1910–1935

•

The Loew Building, New York City (Palisades Amusement Park Historical Society)

conglomerate: Metro-Goldwyn-Mayer. Loew's right-hand man in the merger deal was Nicholas Schenck.

While the Schenck brothers were making motion picture history, the Park flourished during the "carefree" decade of the twenties. Its mammoth swimming pool (and the Schencks' connections in Tinseltown) attracted scores of celebrities: Gallagher and Shean (the second half of which, Al Shean, was a maternal uncle to the Marx Brothers), the Ziegfeld Follies' Girls, Babe Ruth, Jack Dempsey,

The Park on the Palisades (Cliffside Park Free Public Library)

Above, left. Swimmers at the diving board (*The Palisadian*)

Above, right. Charleston contests were held regularly during the twenties. (*The Palisadian*)

Buster Keaton, W. C. Fields, and Jackie Coogan. The Park also featured the finest in entertainment—including Charles Strickland and his ten-piece jazz orchestra, which performed regularly in the dance hall.

Nothing stood in the way of the Park's success. When a strike in August 1923 stopped the trolley system in its tracks, Palisades acquired 260 sightseeing buses to carry its patrons from every ferry and every town within twenty-five miles of the Park. Palisades Amusement Park became so popular that the nearby town of Palisades Park, which had been incorporated since 1894, made public its desire to change its name because of the many instances of misdirected mail and misled visitors. (Those asking for directions to Palisades Park were usually sent to the amusement park instead of the town.)

In 1924 the Park featured infant incubators that were monitored by a medical doctor. Incubators in an amusement resort were not a unique idea—Coney Island had successfully featured incubators for almost twenty years—but the public remained fascinated by the medical wonder of it all.

The Park also headlined the most unusual acts in the country. Daisy and Violet Hilton, the San Antonio Siamese twins, plunged into the salty waters of the pool while newsreel and newspaper cameras captured the event. The Great Sir Joseph Ginzberg, billed

Top. Daisy and Violet Hilton (*The Palisadian*)

Above. Population Charlie (*The Palisadian*)

as "The World's Worst Entertainer," sang "Asleep in the Deep" and six or seven hundred other songs in four distinct voices. And Population Charlie just stood on stage and recited populations. Charlie knew the correct population of every town in the United States that had five thousand or more residents. The audience at Palisades was invited to shout out the name of a town, and Charlie would give the population. Or the audience could give the population and Charlie would name the town. He also would name its leading hotels, the number of rooms each hotel had, and the distance from the town to the nearest city. He knew the exact height of all the major bridges in the country and the dates of more than two thousand inventions, plus a wealth of other trivia. He even astonished professors in a three-hour session at Columbia University in 1925, when they tried to stump him with a series of hard questions. The prior year, he had equally amazed the faculty at the University of Southern California.

By this time, commercial radio was in its infancy (the report of the 1920 election results by Station KDKA in Pittsburgh is generally considered the start of professional broadcasting) and Palisades Amusement Park did not ignore this growing phenomenon. In 1924 radio history took place when an army airplane flying over the Park communicated with a New York broadcast station, WHN, that had set up a transmission site on the Park grounds. This was the first ground-to-air transmission ever made.

Pilot: "Here we are folks, right over the Park about at an altitude of four thousand feet. You can't possibly see us but we can see you. It seems as though there were a million electric light bulbs down where you are and the saltwater pool glistens like a jewel."

Nils T. Granlun (WHN broadcaster): "Can you hear me talking?"

Pilot: "Just as though you were sitting in the plane, and what's more, we can hear Charlie Strickland's music coming from the dance hall."

N.T.G.: (*crowd cheers loudly*)

Pilot: "We are about through for the evening, folks, so we bid you good night. We have turned the plane toward Long Island and will land at Mitchell Field in a few minutes—good night."

N.T.G.: "Thank you very much."

Pilot: "We are sure you are very welcome."

Two years later the Park built its own radio station, WPAP, which for many years would broadcast live entertainment from the Park to thousands of metropolitan listeners. The Clarence Williams Trio, the Charles Strickland Orchestra, Eva Taylor, and Mildred Hunt

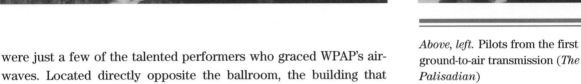

Above, left. Pilots from the first ground-to-air transmission (*The Palisadian*)

Above, right. Charles Strickland (*The Palisadian*)

were just a few of the talented performers who graced WPAP's air-waves. Located directly opposite the ballroom, the building that housed the station was shaped like a huge Atwater-Kent radio. The facility reportedly cost more than $100,000 to build.

The "Roaring Twenties" also marked a boom in thrill rides throughout the amusement industry. The age of the "scream machine" was born, and by the end of the decade there would be nearly thirteen hundred wooden coasters across the United States. To help feed the public's demand for faster, more violent rides, Palisades constructed a massive coaster named the Skyrocket in 1926. Designed by John Miller with assistance from Erwin Vettel, this roller coaster proved to be very popular with the public. Reportedly one hundred feet high at its peak, it was proclaimed by experts as the "latest and greatest ride of its kind in existence."

In 1927, following a fire damaging the Skyrocket, the Park built a new steel coaster called the Cyclone, a nickname for the Traver Giant Cyclone Safety Coaster. This was one of three such thrillers built by Harry Traver, one of the world's most respected roller coaster designers. (His others were the Cyclone at Crystal Beach, Canada, and the Lightning at Revere Beach, Massachusetts.) Between them, the coasters set a new standard for terror. Built near the edge of the cliffs, the one at Palisades was perhaps the most intense; its tight turns (due to the Park's space constraints) and the area's irregular, rocky terrain often made for a rigorous ride. Also, unlike its wooden counterparts, the Cyclone was made of steel—a characteristic that made it even more devastating, since it had no give at all.

The Hollywood Connection, 1910–1935

•

Above, left. Johnny "Freckles" Devine receiving his loving cup from Nicholas Schenck (*The Palisadian*)

Above, right. Crowd watches one of the sensational daredevil acts at the Park (John and Margaret Winkler)

The Cyclone developed so frightful a reputation that people were genuinely afraid to ride it. This, plus frequent maintenance and ever-increasing insurance costs, led to its dismantling in 1934. (The Revere Beach coaster had been taken down a year earlier, and the one at Crystal Beach was dismantled in 1946.)

During these years, Nick Schenck became more involved in his Hollywood career, but he still attempted to keep his name linked with the Park through frequent publicity stunts. One such stunt in 1925 involved a six-year-old youngster named Johnny "Freckles" Devine. According to the *Palisadian* newspaper, Johnny and his family were visiting the Park one day when Nick asked the boy if he thought he could swim across the Hudson River. "Sure I can," snapped Johnny. Schenck promised the boy anything in the Park if he succeeded. Johnny's wish was "all the hot dogs I can eat, all the waffles, too, and then I want to ride on the Motor Parkway for an hour straight." To sweeten the pot, Schenck promised to add "a solid silver loving cup."

The deal was struck, and Schenck made sure that every news organization was present to capture the event. On the afternoon of August 31, two dozen cameramen snapped the boy as Johnny began his three-quarter-mile journey from the 135th Street pier in Manhattan. A circling current pulled the feisty youth downriver. His father,

★ ★

The Perils of Palisades

Although Palisades Amusement Park prospered during the Roaring Twenties, the decade was also fraught with accidents. In 1920 the Park's first major fire destroyed one of the oldest pavilions in the Park, Mrs. Noffka's restaurant. In August 1924, a man suffered a heart attack while diving into the saltwater pool and died. Five years later, another died after bumping his head on the pool's diving board. In 1926, a woman was killed when she fell from a car on the newly installed Skyrocket roller coaster. The following season, the Skyrocket was among several rides partly destroyed by fire.

One of the worst disasters occurred in May 1928, when a thunderous noise rocked the towns of Fort Lee and Cliffside Park. The fireworks displays, stored in two sheds near the huge sign on the cliffs, had exploded. Scores of windows near the area were shattered and one wall of the shed was blown over the cliffs. The eighteen-foot letters that spelled out PALISADES AMUSEMENT PARK were damaged, leaving ferry passengers with only a partial message. Three women in Edgewater entered into nervous shock. Others at the base of the cliffs became hysterical, believing the rocks of the Palisades were tumbling upon them. Although the cause of the accident was never determined, the most popular theory was that the shed had been sabotaged by a rival fireworks manufacturer; its walls had blown inward, indicating an explosive device had been ignited on the outside. Amazingly, there was only one fatality. Shortly before the blast, the man in charge of the pyrotechnics displays, Joseph Barnaba, sent his eighteen-year-old son, Nicholas, to the back of the shed to get one of the frames used for ground displays. Nicholas was killed in the explosion.

Firemen view the rubble of the fireworks shed, May 1928 (*The Palisadian*)

While all of these accidents generated the kind of bad publicity that would have put most other enterprises out of business, the Schencks were, through their Hollywood connections, able to dilute the effects by calling on the day's celebrities. For example, in June 1927, New Jersey resident hero Charles Lindbergh flew his plane up the Hudson while Palisades, in salute, provided a daylight display of fireworks; huge aerial bombs burst among the heavens and released American flags. And in 1928 a casting call for 326 youngsters went out when movie director Hal Roach came to the Park to audition children for roles in his new *Our Gang* comedy features.

★ ★

Cartoon published in *The Palisadian*, May 1926. The caption reads: "Near-sighted old gentleman (who has gotten on the scenic railway by mistake): 'Er—excuse me, but this is right for Times Square, isn't it?'"

on one of the many boats following Johnny, shouted words of encouragement. Within thirty-five minutes, the boy reached the New Jersey shore. Upon returning to the Park, he was presented with the loving cup. For four memorable hours, Johnny had the time of his life; the Park was his. And Nick Schenck received a million dollars' worth of free publicity.

Despite such efforts, Schenck's Hollywood endeavors were allowing him less and less time to devote to Palisades Amusement Park. Though probably not evident to visitors at the Park, the employees soon came to realize that the Schencks were an ownership in name only.

Then, on September 25, 1927, the Schencks' long-time friend and business partner, Marcus Loew, died. The presidency of Loew's empire passed on to his chief lieutenant, Nicholas. That same year Joseph was elected president of United Artists, and he became one of the original founders of the Motion Picture Academy of Arts and Sciences. Movie-going had become a national obsession. By the end of the decade, more than twenty-one thousand ornate motion picture palaces were located across the country, and it was estimated that sixty million Americans had gone to the movies at least once. The Schencks' combined annual income was estimated at $1 million and their total wealth was reported to be in the vicinity of $20 million.

Then, with little more than two months of the twenties remaining, Wall Street pulled the rug out from under the nation's prosperity. October 29—Black Tuesday—marked the start of the Great Depression, and the end of the free-spirited, free-wheeling, and free-spending days.

At the start of the new decade, the Park barely stayed in the black as attendance dropped. The Great Depression had strangled the American spirit that typified the twenties. People still needed diversions, but they didn't have the money to spend. To attract more patrons, the Park offered prizes of food and groceries—a most welcome inducement in those hard times. Coffee and sugar replaced Kewpie dolls.

In 1931, the Park received help in its quest for more patrons. Talk of spanning the Hudson River with a bridge had dated back to as early as 1811. But the rapid growth of automobiles during the 1920s had inspired action, and in December 1931 the newly created Port of New York Authority completed the thirty-five-hundred-foot George Washington Bridge. Suspended more than two hundred feet above the Hudson River, the bridge had taken more than four years to complete at a cost of almost $60 million. The towns on top of the Palisades had always posed two obstacles to travelers: the Hudson River and the mammoth, rocky cliffs. Both obstacles were eliminated with this new bridge, permitting easy access to the area—and to the Park.

By now, Nicholas Schenck was heading an entertainment empire that employed twelve thousand people, and he continued to use his Hollywood talent to beef up the gate at Palisades. Newspa-

The Hollywood Connection, 1910–1935

The swimming pool, July 4, 1934
(*The Record*)

pers exhibited Jean Harlow riding the Park's scenic railroad. Johnny Weismuller, the silver screen's Tarzan, played guest of honor at the 1932 season opening of the pool. Even young Jackie Cooper dropped by to pay a visit.

At the same time, Schenck was battling with the towns of Fort Lee and Cliffside Park, both of which wanted to raise Palisades' license fees. Palisades Amusement Park was the largest local tax asset, and the money it paid was clear profit for the towns since the Park provided for its own police and firefighters, its own street and sewer maintenance, and its own garbage disposal. However, the towns were still foundering from the devastating Depression, and they believed the Park had money to spare. In May 1930 Fort Lee tried to raise the license fee from $1,500 to $5,000; the Park and the town finally settled on $2,000.

Three years later, claiming it had been running in the red, the Park sought a dramatic reduction in the fees. It requested that Fort Lee's $2,000 fee and Cliffside Park's $1,500 fee be reduced to $25 each. To support their case, Park officials noted that they annually paid Fort Lee more than $20,000 and Cliffside about $28,000 in real and personal property taxes. These figures influenced the two towns

Above, left and right. Frolicking on the sand beach and in the pool, ca. 1930 (Mr. and Mrs. M. Peragine)

Below. The swimming pool; waterfalls on the left, July 4, 1934 (*The Record*)

Nicholas Schenck (*The Palisadian*)

to reduce their fees to $500 each. Less than six weeks later, the Park applied to the county for reductions in the assessed valuation. Palisades wanted the Fort Lee property to drop from $182,000 to $36,000, and the property in Cliffside Park to go from $250,000 to $57,000.

The following season—the same year the Park obtained its first beer permit—the battle continued as Cliffside Park returned the Park's $500 check for the license fee and advised it that the fee was once again $1,500. The Park's property assessment was finally settled in June 1934 when the State Board of Tax Appeals set the Cliffside Park property's valuation at $176,725 and Fort Lee's at $101,986.

On May 18, 1934, it was announced that the Schencks had sold a majority of their stock in the Palisade Realty and Amusement Company to New York City attorney Clarence Hand. (They did not completely relinquish control, however; Nicholas's wife, Pansy, held a $500,000 mortgage on the property.) Hand was named the new president of the Park.

The Schencks' power and influence in Hollywood by this time were unquestionable. Joe Schenck and Darryl Zanuck had two years earlier completed the merger of Twentieth Century Pictures and Fox Studios, and Nicholas was finding the returns on his investment in Palisades could scarcely compare to the veritable bonanza he had stumbled upon in the City of Angels. Then, in April 1935, the federal government declared that the Palisades Realty and Trust Company owed the two boroughs $80,000 in back taxes and interest. Rumors soon arose that if Hand's company did not make restitution, Nicholas Schenck would take care of the matter by buying out the company, tearing down the Park, and making it the center of an eastern movie industry. Hand sought to maintain control through a reorganization plan, but it was too late. The matter was finally resolved on May 2, 1935, at a sheriff's auction, when the Schencks bought the property outright with a bid of $150,000.

The plan to turn the Park into an eastern Hollywood never unfolded. Upon acquiring title to the property, the Schencks wanted out. Ferris wheels and roller coasters had lost their appeal for the brothers, who had too much going on in California. Later that May, the Schencks announced they had effected a deal. They had leased the property to another pair of enterprising show business brothers, Jack and Irving Rosenthal.

Evolution
1935-1959

*I*RVING AND JACK Rosenthal, along with six brothers and sisters, grew up in the slums of New York's Lower East Side around the turn of the century. Their father had died in 1896, a week before Irving was born. At six, Irving delivered newspapers to help out the family. Four years later, in an early exhibit of their entrepreneurial spirit, he and twelve-year-old Jack borrowed $45 to buy pails and shovels and another $50 to rent a stand at Steeplechase Park in Coney Island. In an interview later published by *Amusement Park Journal*, Irving recalled, "We were the biggest pail and shovel sellers at the beach that year, and made more than $1,500. It wasn't long before we figured out how to engineer maximum sales. Two excursion boats came in daily from New Jersey. I stood at the end of the pier and handed each child a pail and shovel. Jack stood at the other end of the pier and collected five cents from the parents as they passed him. We didn't miss many sales because by the time the kids got to Jack they weren't going to give up their pails and shovels for anything."

The next year the brothers bought a second concession stand at Coney Island's Luna Park. It lost as much money as their stand in Steeplechase had made. Then in 1908, at Savin Rock Park in West Haven, Connecticut, the brothers bought a souvenir stand and sold felt hats whose brims were embroidered with the patron's name. Their $150 investment paid off.

"We stayed open until the dance hall closed at midnight, and many of the fellows would buy novelties for their girls," Irving said. "We were open again at 8:00 a.m. to catch the early morning arrivals and picnic groups."

As teenagers, Irving and Jack bought a secondhand merry-go-round, which they ran at Savin Rock Park. Other concessionaires watched and waited for the Rosenthals to fail at their feeble attempt to generate a profit from this has-been carousel. They netted $11,000. According to Irving, "There were already two merry-go-rounds at Savin Rock when we installed our unit, and everybody thought we were nuts. But we had it figured out, and our ideas paid off. Instead of one organ, we installed two, and we had two ring-boards. We got new popular music on an exclusive basis for a month, and the whole set-up appealed to the patrons."

The brothers rapidly expanded their holdings at Savin Rock. They erected a shooting gallery, a fun house, various game concessions, and, around 1911, a roller coaster. They also leased the Golden City Park Arena in Canarsie, Brooklyn, and featured free amateur boxing. (This attraction was the predecessor of the Golden Gloves competition begun by the *New York Daily News* in 1927.) They bought a chain of movie theaters that later became the Skouras chain, and they built the Royal York Hotel in Florida, which they sold for a quick profit.

During the twenties, the brothers engaged in different pursuits. Irving graduated from the New York Dental School, while Jack studied the violin and became an accomplished concert master with the Cincinnati Symphony. But the sounds of the carnival midway held a greater attraction for the Rosenthal brothers than did dentist drills and violins. In 1927, at a cost of $146,000, they built and operated the Cyclone coaster at Coney Island.

Still, the Rosenthals needed something bigger, something better. They needed their own park. In 1932 they approached Nick Schenck with an offer to buy Palisades for almost $1.5 million. Schenck declined. Then, in 1935, Nicholas sent for the Rosenthals. The brothers struck a deal to lease the Park with an option to buy. "When we took it over, the Park was losing $80,000 a year and people in the business thought we were nuts," Irving later said.

With Jack serving as showman and Irving providing the business acumen, the brothers set about to turn Palisades into a profitable enterprise. Their niece Anna (who as a young girl worked with her uncles at Savin Rock and later joined them at Golden City Park Arena as the world's first woman boxing promoter) oversaw the Park's employees as general manager. To ensure they received enough press, the brothers hired one of the top publicists of the day,

Irving Rosenthal (*The Palisadian*)

Joe McKee (Aseneath McKee)

Bert Nevins, who previously handled public relations for Coney Island's Luna Park. Nevins's greatest assets were his newsreel connections; in the world of public relations, movie newsreels were held in the highest esteem as more and more people sought to forget the Depression by escaping into the fantasies of the silver screen.

The brothers also employed Joe McKee as the Park's superintendent. Affectionately nicknamed "Roller Coaster Joe," McKee was one of the few roller coaster craftsmen in the world. He started his vocation in 1905, working at the old Luna Park in Pittsburgh, Pennsylvania, and over the years he designed rides that thrilled people from Paris to New Orleans. McKee developed many safety devices for his rides, such as the lock-in safety device that kept coaster trains on the track. "Each car is locked in its tracks by twelve wheels and can't be removed except at the entrance or loading stop. You can bet the ride is safe," McKee once bragged to the *Bergen Record*. The device became standard on all coasters—and, as with his other safety features, he shared it with the industry without compensation. McKee became so highly respected that he was named consultant to Lloyds of London for thrill-ride insurance.

The Park opened under the new management in May 1935. Interestingly, the previous year's weekend admission fare of fifteen cents had been lowered to ten cents—the first indication of the Rosenthals' generosity-in-business schemes.

It seemed through May and June that, with the back taxes paid off and the capable Rosenthals in charge, the Park was squarely back on track. But on July 1, with ten thousand people in attendance, something happened that no one could have foreseen.

That afternoon, in the northeast section of the Park, the orange glow of snapping flames appeared; later speculation proposed they had started when someone dropped a lit cigarette on the dried wood of the Old Mill, a ride that had been built in 1924. Concessionaires tried in vain to extinguish the fire, which spread rapidly as it fed on the dry timber of nearby pavilions. Thousands watched from neighboring communities as the flames rose skyward, and traffic jams across the river lined New York's Riverside Drive from Seventy-second Street to the Dyckman Street Ferry. Fire companies arrived, and volunteers from the crowd helped them to guide the Park's patrons to safety. When the fire hit the shooting gallery, ammunition began to pop; firefighters and spectators had to duck behind trees and fences to evade the ricocheting pellets.

Fed by an easterly wind, the flames mounted. They engulfed the Whip and devoured the Creation, an exhibit that depicted the history of life. Finally, at six o'clock that evening, the fire was smothered;

Above, left and right. Firefighters battle the flames, July 2, 1935. (*Fire Engineering Magazine* and Memories Restaurant)

Left. Flames rise from the Park. (*The Record*)

the smoldering embers were doused by water, until each one had been totally extinguished. Nineteen people— including 11 of the 125 firefighters on the scene—had been injured, and at least one person had been shot in the hand by a pellet from the shooting gallery. About one-eighth of the Park lay in ruins, and the cost of the damage amounted to $150,000—the biggest losses being the Old Mill and the roller skating rink, valued at $25,000 and $20,000, respectively. Three other buildings and eleven concessions were also destroyed, includ-

Top, right. Roast beef stand lies in ruins. (*The Record*)

Below, right. Pumper truck is backed into the pool. (*The Record*)

ing the Creation exhibit, the shooting gallery, the Whip ride, the Motor Parkway, and several concessions and storerooms. Workers immediately began cleaning up the debris, and the Park reopened that same night. (The fire, however, had at least one unforeseen side effect: Arthur C. Holden, the Park's sixty-six-year-old high diver, dived one hundred feet into a pool that had earlier been siphoned to help fight the conflagration. Though the depth of the water had been reduced from five to four feet, Holden stood firmly in the tradition of "the show must go on." "I wouldn't disappoint the crowd," he said later. "They gave me a swell ovation.")

Ever the showman, Holden takes the plunge. (*The Palisadian*)

In August, the Rosenthal brothers exercised their option to buy and paid the Schencks $450,000. That same month they announced that several new additions were being added, among them a large athletic field, an expanded beach for the pool, picnic grounds, and a children's playground, which would become known as Kiddieland.

The 1936 season boasted a new Water Scooter ride—the largest of its kind in the country—in which patrons were able to pilot red-and-white boats powered by gas engines. The facade of the new ride resembled a huge steamship, and all the attendants were dressed in sailor suits. This ride, as well as other new additions, helped to draw patrons to the Park. However, the Rosenthals also knew the value of advertising. That August, construction began on a new billboard for the cliffs. The sign was 24 feet high and 240 feet long, and its 32,000 electric light bulbs scrolled advertising messages that could easily be read by the people in Manhattan. Reportedly the largest moving sign in the world, it became a landmark on the cliffs.

That season was also marked by less-than-welcome events. In May, police thwarted a Park publicity stunt in which Chicago high diver Viola Moss, clad in the latest beach attire, attempted to dive off the George Washington Bridge. (A year earlier, Arthur Holden had attempted the same stunt but had also been stopped before he could leap.) The police arrested Miss Moss as well as Bert Nevins and Park

A billboard in Manhattan advertising the "World's Finest Playground" (Memories Restaurant)

announcer Clem White, both of whom had accompanied the high diver. All three were charged with disorderly conduct and fined $25 or five days in jail, and the judge said he was going to stop people from using the bridge for cheap publicity.

Two months later, six monkeys escaped from Monkey Island, a Park exhibit that allowed children to stare in wonder at the simian antics. During a change in the surrounding moat's water, the clever monkeys used the hose that had emptied the moat to climb up the retaining wall. They immediately took to the streets. By the end of the week, only three of the six escapees had been returned; two had been recovered in trees, and one was found in a local bakery, eating to his heart's content. The other three were never found.

And, of course, the new owners faced the same old complaints as area residents protested the screaming and screeching that came from the roller coaster. In June, Cliffside Park officials introduced an ordinance that would force the roller coaster to close down at 11:00 p.m. on weekday nights and Sundays, and at midnight on Saturdays. However, fearing a possible lawsuit from the Rosenthals, the officials took no action on the new law until after the 1936 season ended. Then the town passed an even stricter mandate that not only restricted the operation of the coaster, but also directed that shooting galleries, loudspeakers, and "any other noise-producing contrivance" not be used after the appointed hours.

Despite this law, in 1937 the Park constructed a new coaster called the Lake Placid Bobsled. Built by John Miller—the same man who earlier constructed the Skyrocket—this was the tallest of the flying-turn coasters. Unlike traditional coasters that were mounted on a set of tracks, flying-turn coasters ran on swiveling rubber wheels. They would race down chutes and around steeply banked turns, sometimes being perpendicular to the ground. The Lake Placid Bobsled was considered the most vicious of this type of coaster. Its lift hill proved so intimidating that the climb was enclosed to prevent passengers from looking down. Extra side wheels and channels of reinforced concrete were essential to keep the riders from being badly shaken. The Bobsled was destined to follow the fate of the original Traver Cyclone, however, as low ridership and high maintenance eventually led to its dismantling.

The next season marked the end of a more sedate ride. The old Bergen County trolley reached the end of its line in 1938, as buses had become the transportation of the masses. The railway system had served the area well since the turn of the century. It had provided an inexpensive means of transportation, easily accessible, and it was perhaps the most instrumental factor in the development of this suburban area. But the trolley system was slow, and it had failed to adapt to the changing times. The growing popularity of the automobile, improved state highways, and the opening of the George Washington Bridge combined to bring about the end of the rail system. The period between 1926 and 1938 saw more and more sections of the trolley line discontinue service, until the entire system finally closed down on August 5, 1938.

To keep the people coming to the former trolley park, Bert Nevins that year started the Mrs. America Pageant. Wedded beauties from all sections of New Jersey, Connecticut, upper New York State, Pennsylvania, and Delaware vied for the coveted title. Regionals were held at Palisades, with the finals taking place in Asbury Park. He also concocted the Eyeglass-wearing Beauty Pageant in 1941, open only to bespectacled beauties.

In 1938 Nevins was again arrested, along with the Rosenthals and several other Park employees, for operating what was described as a "Slave Market." The charge stemmed from an attraction in which men and women were matched up in a style similar to that of a dating service, though with no commission fees or admission charges. The Park defended the show as "an entirely human interest

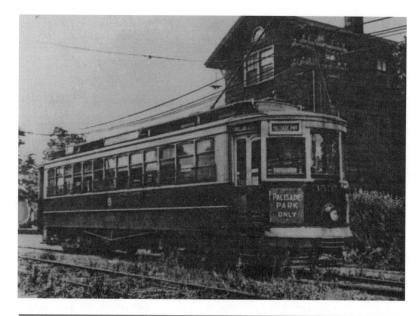

Left. Eyeglass-wearing beauty contestant (*The Palisadian*)

Above. Prior to 1938, special trolleys were run in the summer to the Park. (Edgewater Free Public Library)

attraction" and denied it had acted as a "marriage brokerage agency." The arrests generated great press coverage for the Park, all of it free, before a Bergen County Grand Jury in November cleared the Park and all of the people arrested of any wrongdoing. (One of those arrested, Adolph Schwartz, later caused his own bit of controversy by operating the popular Mouse Game. A live mouse scampered across a board rimmed by thirty-six holes, and patrons bet on the hole into which the mouse would disappear. The game was discontinued in the mid-forties in the interest of the welfare of the mice.)

However, the public outcry against the morals of the Park could not compare to the turbulent unrest spreading throughout Western Europe. It had been called the European Conflict by uninterested Americans. By 1939, it had presented an annoying encroachment on overseas trade. By December 7, 1941, it was a global nightmare as the Japanese attacked Pearl Harbor and the United States was thrown headlong into World War II.

The Park tried to play down the war and instead offer a place to escape the world's problems. Yet every citizen, every company, and every industry had to do its part in the war effort. Palisades Amusement Park proved no exception.

Above, left. Patrons gather at the prize wheel (Memories Restaurant)

Above, right. Happy faces on the roller coaster (Memories Restaurant)

Left. One popular game on the midway was the cigarette wheel. A sign on the wall reads: "Obey your air raid warden. We have provided for your safety. BE CALM—DON'T RUN—Walk to the north east N.Y. gate." (Bob Nesoff)

The Park conducted regular blackout drills and offered a special season membership for families of defense workers. It gave out $1,000 War Bonds as prizes for the beauty pageants. Even its attractions reflected the mood of the era with a ride called MacArthur's Bombers and a show called the Swing Shift Frolics, which boasted talented war-plant workers. In 1943, an attraction called Bundles for Buddies enabled patrons to win special packages that would be sent to the boys in service. And soldiers in uniform were always admitted into Palisades free, a policy that would continue for the remainder of the Park's existence.

Enjoying a ride on the Virginia Reel
(John and Margaret Winkler)

Palisades Amusement Park, far from the front lines, couldn't have seemed more distant from disaster. Yet on August 13, 1944, fire once again found its way into the Park, in what would prove to be one of the worst conflagrations in local history.

The Virginia Reel was a popular amusement ride throughout the United States during the early 1940s, and the one at Palisades Park was no exception. Passengers rode in a series of tubs, each one large enough to carry at least eight people. The tubs whirled their way along curving tracks, down steep inclines, and through dark tunnels.

On the Sunday afternoon of August 13, one boy's voice rose above the passengers' laughter: "It's smoking!" The boy's name was Charlie Larkin, and, by all accounts, it was the last thing he ever said.

"Don't worry," the ride attendant responded, "there's nothing wrong." Less than a minute later, the Virginia Reel erupted in flames.

Those who could escape, did. Those who were less fortunate, like the group of people riding through one of the Virginia Reel's darkened tunnels, found themselves engulfed in flames.

Panic swept through the Park as the wind carried the flames to new heights. Some patrons stopped whatever they were doing to investigate the commotion, while others ran for the exits. Those in the pool—an estimated four thousand people—were forced to evacuate without retrieving their clothing; they had no alternative but to observe the blaze from the street dressed in their swimsuits. Police had to restrain parents searching for missing children and others

Left. Intense flames devoured this Virginia Reel car and its passengers (John and Margaret Winkler)

Below. Boy watches as smoke engulfs airplane ride (*The Record*)

Evolution, 1935–1959

•

Top, right. Smoke fills the midways (Thomas Leahy)

Below, right. Exhausted firefighters (*The Record*)

searching for lost belongings. One woman with a camera kept a cooler vigil. As the flames grew higher, twenty-one-year-old Agnes Hayek climbed onto one of the pool's ten-foot-high diving boards and began snapping photographs.

"At first it was unbelievable," she later recounted for the *New York Times*. "Just minutes before, people had been laughing and enjoying the day, and now there was utter panic everywhere. The rides looked like a bunch of straw going up. The Shoot-the-Chute went up like paper."

The spectacle must have seemed like an illustration from Dante's Inferno. Monstrous flames swept through the center of the Park as people ran in all directions. Thousands watched from across the river as parts of the gigantic Skyrocket coaster, its timbers cracking and snapping, came crashing down like a toppled dinosaur, shooting sparks in every direction. Sirens blared, spectators screamed, explosions went off like cannon fire. Gasoline tanks exploded as the fire reached the parking lot; more than half of the two hundred vehicles were devoured by the blaze. The heat was so intense that tires melted into puddles of rubber.

Nurses and medics, hearing a broadcast for help from the Park's own radio station, hurried to the scene. Red Cross and other first aid stations were set up around the Park. Police were aided by Civilian Defense volunteers in eliminating traffic snarls. Firemen from fourteen municipalities arrived to fight the blaze. (In one instance, a pumper truck was backed up to the edge of the pool, which had become a handy source of water. When flames neared the truck, firefighters backed it *into* the pool in an attempt to save it. The corrosive effects of the saltwater, however, caused its own irreparable damage.)

During its two-hour advancement, the fire consumed the Skyrocket, the carousel, the Virginia Reel, the Small Scenic Railway (a tamer version of the Big Scenic), the Snapper, the fun house, the glass house, the dancing pavilion, and most of the concessions along the midways. The administration building and the Casino restaurant were also destroyed. It was the greatest carnage in the area's history. Yet, to the credit of the fire departments, only seven people—those who had been caught in the Virginia Reel—were killed. One hundred and fifty others were badly injured. The cost of the destruction was estimated at $1 million.

Despite a stringent investigation, the exact cause of the fire was never ascertained. It was rumored that Park maintenance men used kerosene to clean the tracks of the rides, then threw the rags onto litter piles in storage sheds—one of which was located directly under the Virginia Reel. The most prevalent speculation was that friction on the hoisting cable of the Virginia Reel had produced airborne sparks, igniting the rags and the structure's wood like tinder. The bone-dry weather—the summer of '44 delivered a record-breaking drought that had already caused major fires in Hoboken and at Coney Island—only aggravated the situation.

When it was over, the complaints came as furiously as the fire itself. Walter G. Winnie, a Bergen County prosecutor, was severe in his deprecations: "There was a total and shocking absence of

Top, left. A nearby car consumed by fire (Thomas Leahy)

Top, right. Cars in the parking lot are destroyed. (Thomas Leahy)

Above. Over half the park was turned into rubble. (Cliffside Park Free Public Library)

Below, left. Tires melted from the heat. (John and Margaret Winkler)

Below, right. Destroyed pumper truck (*The Record*)

Palisades Amusement Park

•

Above, left. The area near the swimming pool (John and Margaret Winkler)

Above, right. Skyrocket coaster after the fire (*The Record*)

Below. Trees, older than the Park itself, fall victim to the fire. (Cliffside Park Free Public Library)

Evolution, 1935–1959
•

Above, left. Patrons search in the parking lot for any trace of their cars. (Cliffside Park Free Public Library)

Above, right. Construction was started almost immediately on a new home for the carousel. (John and Margaret Winkler)

thought in regard to fire prevention in the construction of this park. There was fire-fighting equipment, but it was untried and inadequate! And there was a total lack of personnel trained to make use of this equipment."

Despite this rebuke, in October a grand jury cleared the Park of any responsibility for the fire. By then the reconstruction had already begun. Permits had been quickly issued by Cliffside Park and Fort Lee, and the Rosenthals had received priority for war-rationed items such as wood, rubber, and steel because the Park was considered "recreation" for the servicemen.

The bases of the reconstructed buildings now used cinder block and other fireproof materials, and a new water main was installed to facilitate fire fighting. Buildings and rides were rebuilt, including:

- **Skyrocket / Cyclone Coasters.** The 1944 fire marked the third time the Skyrocket was the victim of flames. The ride was redesigned, and its reconstruction was supervised by Joe McKee himself. Once complete, the new coaster was ceremoniously renamed the Cyclone. A traditional wooden structure, this became one of the most thrilling rides in the Park and one of the most famous coasters in the world.
- **Carousel.** The new building featured thick walls and a domed roof, and was surrounded by a strip of food and candy concessions that became known as Candyland. It also housed a new

Above, left. The heavily damaged fun house is reconstructed. (John and Margaret Winkler)

Above, right. Midways, destroyed by fire, await reconstruction. (John and Margaret Winkler)

Left. Workers begin the massive job of cleanup. (John and Margaret Winkler)

Below. The fun house was reconstructed during the winter of '44-'45, and ready for opening the next spring. (John and Margaret Winkler)

Evolution, 1935–1959

•

Penny arcade owner Philip Mazzocchi (Joan Mazzocchi-Lagasi and Pier Lagasi)

carousel purchased from the Philadelphia Toboggan Company. Originally manufactured in 1928, the carousel had operated at Happyland Hastings Park in Vancouver, British Columbia, Canada until 1934. It was then moved to Old Orchard Beach, Maine, where it remained until the Philadelphia Toboggan Company reconditioned it for Palisades. With a base that was fifty-two feet wide, it featured sixty-four horses—including forty jumpers—two chariots, and more than one thousand lights.

- **Penny Arcade.** The Penny Arcade, housed in a new brick building, occupied what had been the site of the Virginia Reel. The arcade's owner, Philip Mazzocchi, had originally run a grocery store; in 1915, he and a friend, August Berni, opened a Skee-ball concession at Palisades and began a long association with the amusement park. The two men built the arcade into a lucrative business over the years. (Every day, Philip appeared at work in a smart suit that he then covered with an apron to keep clean.) The fire destroyed everything. In fact, the heat had been so intense that, when Mazzocchi recovered the safe from the ashes, he found the dollar bills charred beyond recognition and the silver coins melted into a clump.

Like the legendary Phoenix, Palisades Amusement Park rose from its ashes. By the end of the following year, the mightiest, most terrible war in the history of civilization was over. Unlike the rest of the world, the thirty-eight-acre park recovered from its ordeal swiftly and efficiently.

JACK ROSENTHAL had kept a low profile after the 1944 fire. He had been stricken with Parkinson's disease, which would slowly steal away his health. Irving was now taking a more public stance as the Park's popularity grew. With the war over, a carefree attitude had overtaken the country. Time seemed more precious now; "Enjoy life, it's later than you think" was the catch-phrase of the day. Returning soldiers went on a spending spree nationwide. Their taste in amusement rides had become more sophisticated, and the thrill rides became faster than ever. Boyfriends and girlfriends were tearfully reunited, and husbands and wives were given a second chance to fall in love. The Old Mill, a ride originally known as the Mill on the Floss, featured boats floating through shadowy caverns, and it became a perfect meeting place for romantic couples. Palisades renamed the ride the Tunnel of Love, and amusement parks throughout the country followed suit.

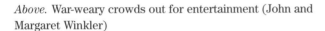

Above. War-weary crowds out for entertainment (John and Margaret Winkler)

Right. The Carousel (John and Margaret Winkler)

The Park seemed impervious to bad publicity. Though it continued to be plagued by occasional accidents—a father who died after falling from the Ferris wheel; two men who were killed when a cable snapped on a whirling aerial ride, the Flying Scooter, sending one of the cars crashing into the crowd—business was better than ever. In June 1946 a novel wedding at the Park captured this national mood. Alfred J. Schiebel of Weehawken married Anne Monaco of Jersey City, and the entire ceremony took place on the carousel. The bride and groom repeated their vows while whirling around on wooden horses. (Shortly after the ceremony, the Council of Churches, Cliffside Park Area, issued a lengthy statement in the *The Palisadian* newspaper, calling the affair "irreverent holding in disrespect both of the sacredness of the religious conception of marriage and the honor due to law and order under the State.")

Of course, life was not carefree for all Americans. Inarguably, blacks had been fighting a war of their own for more than two hundred years. In the summer of 1946, that war hit Bergen County and, specifically, Palisades Amusement Park.

The Park operated what it called the Sun and Surf Club; only members of this club were admitted into the saltwater pool. In reality, the club allowed Park officials to discriminate according to the color of a patron's skin. In July 1946, ten people, eight black and two white, visited the Park as a group. The two whites were sold tickets for the swimming pool while all the blacks were refused admission.

Evolution, 1935–1959
•

Top. The penny arcade (Joan Mazzocchi-Lagasi and Pier Lagasi)

Above, left. The midways of the Park were kept immaculate. (Rich Hanley)

Above, right. The entrance from the parking lot (Rich Hanley)

Right. Crowds packed the Park (John and Margaret Winkler)

Palisades Amusement Park

●

Above, left. Lines outside the gate of Palisades Amusement Park (P. J. Shelley/CPHS yearbook)

Above, right. American Legion raffles a 1947 Ford to raise money. (*The Palisadian*)

The following month, the American Civil Liberties Union requested the Bergen County Grand Jury to investigate the Park's admission policy for the pool. This was the beginning of a controversy that would drag on for several seasons. By the time the Park closed for 1946, the grand jury still had not acted upon the petition from the ACLU. But the Rosenthals' hopes that the issue would disappear from the headlines were swiftly shattered the following season.

On the morning of July 13, 1947, a twenty-two-year-old black woman from New York, Melba Valle, was given a pool ticket by a white friend. When she tried to use it, though, she was refused admission on the grounds that she was not a club member. No shrinking violet, Valle returned later in the day with a group of blacks and whites representing the Congress of Racial Equality (CORE) and Modern Trend. They vowed to return every Sunday until blacks were permitted entrance to the pool. Irving Rosenthal suspended all ticket sales that afternoon, claiming the pool was too crowded. This marked the beginning of a long and bitter feud.

Several dozen protestors, both black and white, converged on the Park each Sunday and handed out leaflets that read in part, "Don't Get Cool at Palisades Pool . . . Get Your Relaxation Where There's No Discrimination!" After several weeks, police were brought in; their presence only added to the already tense atmosphere. On August 3 a fray led to eleven arrests, seven by Fort Lee

and four by Cliffside Park police. The next week, six more people
were arrested for disorderly conduct. The Worker's Defense League
filed a federal suit on behalf of Valle against Palisades Park, seeking
$270,000 in damages. They also requested the FBI's help to investi-
gate charges of discrimination, unlawful arrests, and police brutality.
League officials pointed out that the Bergen County prosecutor was

DON'T GET COOL
AT PALISADES POOL

Palisades Pool, in violation of the New Jersey Civil Rights Law, bars Negroes and persons with dark skins. Such a person is told that a club exists and only members can use the pool. Yet white persons who are not 'members' are regularly admitted and then handed a 'membership' card inside.

Irving Rosenthal, the *Park's owner*, refuses to cease racial discrimination, although it violates the *New Jersey law*. Members of our interracial group who tried peacefully to gain admittance to the pool have been manhandled by the Park's private guards and by Fort Lee police.

On July 27, a Negro was blackjacked from behind by a park representative while other park 'goons' were shoving him on a bus. On August 3, eleven of us were arrested on trumped up charges and two were beaten by the police.

The time has come to end this reign of terror.

By staying away from Palisades Park YOU can help. When the pool is free from discrimination, we can *all* enjoy it.

GET YOUR RELAXATION
WHERE THERE'S
NO DISCRIMINATION!

a member of the law firm representing the amusement park, and that one of the Cliffside Park police had stated to a member of CORE, "Injuring the management's business constitutes disorderly conduct. . . . If I were the owner, I would have your group beaten up or killed."

The presence of the FBI in this small community led to local speculation that white Communists were paying the blacks $15 each to protest and stir up trouble in these Cold War times. These allegations, however, proved unfounded.

Those convicted vowed to appeal, some filed discrimination suits against the Park, and every Sunday there were people loudly voicing their points of view at the gates of Palisades. The trouble even extended across the Hudson. On August 31, while nineteen men and women representing CORE were arrested at Palisades Amusement Park, nine others from the organization were arrested in New York City as they made their voices heard at the entrance to the 125th Street ferry, a popular means of transportation to the Park.

The feud continued throughout the 1948 season. To tone down the controversial publicity, the Rosenthals that year celebrated the

The North Gate at the Park (Cliffside Park Free Public Library)

Golden Jubilee of Palisades Amusement Park. Special events took place weekly to commemorate the anniversary. (Naturally, one of the beauty pageants that year was "The Queen of the Golden Jubilee.") The entire Park was decorated in gold paint, and the hundreds of thousands of electric lights throughout the grounds were interspersed with specially painted gold bulbs. Fireworks, discontinued since the war, were resumed every Tuesday night. The Park even duplicated the popular balloon ascensions to commemorate their first fifty years.

The Rosenthals' Golden Jubilee celebration kept the crowds coming throughout the year, while every Sunday protesters continued to march at the main gates of the Park. In June, the District Court in East Rutherford dismissed the charges of discrimination against the Rosenthals. This action led to more turmoil, and by the following month the protesters were once again in the news when twenty-two people blocked the entrance to the Sun and Surf Club. When they were told to disperse, they insisted on being arrested. They all were charged with disorderly conduct. Six weeks later, another eight protestors were charged with the same offense.

As the new decade rolled in, blacks were finally permitted to swim in the waters of the pool. The Park kept the news very low key;

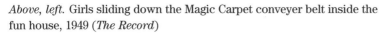

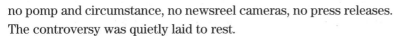

Above, left. Girls sliding down the Magic Carpet conveyer belt inside the fun house, 1949 (*The Record*)

Above, right. Nuns shoot hoops (Memories Restaurant)

Right. Nun tries her skill at the high striker concession, 1953. (*The Record*)

no pomp and circumstance, no newsreel cameras, no press releases. The controversy was quietly laid to rest.

The 1950s brought days of easy affluence to the Park on the Palisades. While the decade has often been called the Fabulous Fifties, a more appropriate moniker might be the Family Fifties. In the postwar climate, men and women seemed more eager to marry, buy a home, and have children. It seemed there were children everywhere, and these Baby Boomers, as they came to be called, filled the Park in record numbers as the decade progressed.

The Park's popularity was undoubtedly aided by an alliance the Rosenthals formed in 1950 with a young Irish immigrant, Morgan "Mickey" Hughes. The son of a working-class couple in Dublin, Hughes joined the Irish Brigade when he was only fifteen. For more than a decade, he fought on the battlefields of Spain, North Africa, Sicily, Italy, France, and Germany. He rose to the rank of major before being discharged in 1949 at the age of thirty.

Hughes had a great love for amusement parks. He especially

Morgan "Mickey" Hughes (Memories Restaurant)

loved the rides, and his travels throughout Europe had allowed him to see some of the world's greatest. When his military service ended, Mickey and a friend purchased the Rotor (later renamed the Magnadrome), a centrifugal ride in which its occupants stood against the walls as it began to spin. As the Rotor's speed increased, the floor would drop away, leaving the dizzy riders pinned to the walls. Hughes operated the Rotor at Bellevue Park in Manchester, England, and it was there that Hughes became associated with the famous showman John Ringling North. In 1950, the pair traveled to the United States to introduce a new breed of rides to Americans.

"The first man I met in this country was George Reiser, who ran the Hot Rods at Palisades," Hughes later recalled. "Joe McKee . . . took me home and he cooked me my first meal on this side of the Atlantic. Then I met Irving Rosenthal."

Rosenthal immediately booked the Rotor, and he and Hughes struck a deal in which Palisades became the nation's premier showcase for new rides. Amusement park owners from across the country joined the Palisades patrons in testing the newest European rides (all of which the Park received for free.) Hughes eventually became the nation's largest ride importer, and he and Rosenthal enjoyed a lucrative partnership for many years.

In addition to displaying superior business sense, Rosenthal also showed that he had not lost his touch for publicity. In May 1950

he hired Dr. George Sykes to guarantee that the sun would shine for the entire week leading up to Memorial Day. Dubbed Operation Sunshine, the Park paid the scientist $200 a day to keep away the clouds within a 105-mile radius. Sykes theorized that by broadcasting sounds, light beams, and electromagnetic waves, he could create atmospheric disturbances that would break up and scatter clouds. His equipment included two radios and an assortment of metal sun reflectors. Though not backed by any scientific evidence, Operation Sunshine made for great press. It did not, however, make for great weather; with the exception of Saturday, the entire week proved cloudy, and on Friday it poured.

As attendance at Palisades increased, traffic snarls became major nuisances for Cliffside Park and Fort Lee. The Park had developed a system in which it collected admission fees from patrons before their cars entered the parking lot; this caused traffic to back up onto the main streets for miles in each direction. A Fort Lee councilman eventually suggested that fares be paid *after* the cars were in the lot. Irving Rosenthal agreed, especially since his brother Sam— the family's black sheep, who oversaw the collecting of fares—had allegedly been pilfering funds.

At the end of 1950, another transportation issue made the news when it was announced that ferry service between New York and New Jersey would discontinue. From the first day of the Park's

The ferry stops its service across the Hudson (Edgewater Free Public Library)

opening, the ferry had transported throngs of patrons who clamored to reach the Palisades. But the rising popularity of the automobile had taken its toll; those crossing the Hudson now preferred to use the George Washington Bridge. Still, many Park patrons depended on the ferry, and Park officials believed its demise would dramatically hurt attendance. They and leaders from Jack Frost Sugar, the Ford Motor Company, and other local businesses met with New Jersey Governor Alfred Driscoll to persuade him to restore the ferry service, but they were unsuccessful.

Then, in March, the Rosenthals announced the Park would start its own ferry service, using two diesel-powered yachts that could each accommodate 250 passengers. While the announcement generated plenty of free press, it never came true. Instead, extra buses were added to the Orange & Black bus line that ran between the Park and the city. In the long run, the additional buses actually worked better than the ferry in bringing patrons to the Park.

That year, another longtime tradition came to an end. Although state laws banning games of chance had been on the books for years, they were rarely enforced, and through them Palisades had enjoyed huge profits. These games—particularly the numerous wheel concessions throughout the Park—were so popular that the wait to obtain a concession was reportedly as long as twenty years. Then, in 1951, a South Jersey boardwalk concessionaire refused to pay a $2 fine for running a game of chance. Overnight, these games were ordered closed from Cape May to Sussex counties. For Palisades the effect was devastating; its rows of gaming concessions came to resemble a ghost town.

The Park brought in whatever it could to make up for the lost

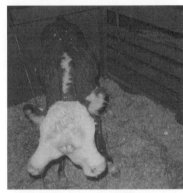

Above, left. The Palace of Illusions (Maie McAskill)

Above, right. Arch and Maie McAskill with their 2 1/4 pound pet dog (Maie McAskill)

Far left. Tom Thumb, the little horse (Maie McAskill)

Left. Two-headed calf (Maie McAskill)

Below. Cow with six legs (Maie McAskill)

★ ★

The Story of Willie Moretti

In October 1951, at Joe's Restaurant on Palisades Avenue (directly across the street from the Park), gangster Willie Moretti was shot dead gangland-style. The restaurant was reportedly a favorite meeting place for mobsters, and the story of Moretti's shooting made front page news from coast to coast.

Many people connected the Park with the event, and decades later they still recounted the Moretti story when reminiscing about Palisades. However, the Park's only connection to the shooting was its location. It is a tribute to the character of Palisades Amusement Park that, even with organized crime so near, it managed to keep it outside of its gates.

★ ★

Sol Abrams (Palisades Amusement Park souvenir book)

revenue. It instituted the Freak Animal Show and the Flea Circus, and Latin American big bands were added to the entertainment roster—including such top talent as the Orchestra Harlow, Nora Moralez, Tito Rodriguez, and Tito Puente.

The Park also helped overcome the cessation of their games of chance through inspired publicity stunts. In 1949, Bert Nevins had handed over the Palisades account to a young, aggressive press agent named Sol Abrams. Abrams subsequently proved his mettle by concocting events that became media bonanzas. One stunt involved the "Swimming Grandma," Betty Cohen, who drew plenty of coverage when she swam from the foot of the Park to the Statue of Liberty. Another involved a young couple who asked to be married on the roller coaster, since that was where they had met; the Park paid for their wedding, which was filmed for newsreels, as well as for a honeymoon at Niagara Falls. But Abrams's greatest stunt occurred around 1956 with the water-skiing circus elephant. Bolted to ten-foot pontoons and pulled by a Mercury-powered motorboat, a $\frac{3}{4}$-ton pachyderm traveled across the Hudson, from New Jersey to the Forty-second Street docks and back, at twenty-five miles an hour, while accompanied by a beautiful showgirl. Photographers from all over the country witnessed the feat, which proved so astonishing that it even pre-empted the annual coverage of the President throwing out the first ball at the Washington Senators' opening game. Such stunts undoubtedly contributed to Abrams being named "one of the ten best press agents in the country" by Pulitzer Prize-winner Jim Bishop in 1960, and to his replacing Bert Nevins as the Park's sole press agent in 1962.

The gambling controversy eventually led to the formation of the New Jersey Amusement Board of Trade (NJABT), which was headed by a Park concessionaire, Joe Weissman. The concessions were changed from "Games of Chance" to "Games of Skill," in which a patron could start and stop the spinning wheels at the press of a button. But through it all, the Park prospered.

By the mid-fifties, the Clyde Beatty Circus had become a regular headliner at Palisades. Beatty, originally associated with Ringling Brothers, had struck out on his own after Ringling closed its tent shows and changed to an indoor format. Many of the featured performers from Ringling Brothers went with Clyde Beatty—including the world's most famous clown, Emmett Kelly, and those death-defying aerialists, the Walendas. Another aerialist, eight-year-old Tito Guilona, later became the star of the show; his performances were highlighted by a triple somersault—a feat that only one other person in the world could accomplish. And Beatty, who billed himself as the world's greatest lion tamer, featured thirteen Nubian lions and Royal Bengal tigers in his act.

The circus opened at the start of each season and ran for six weeks. On a hot summer's day, as the smell of popcorn and roasted peanuts filled the air, children could transport themselves into a world of clowns and gorillas and performing elephants. Eventually, the Clyde Beatty Circus combined with the Hamid Morton Circus (one of whose owners also owned the Steel Pier in Atlantic City), and this new troupe was later replaced by the Hunt Brothers Circus. Despite these changes, the circus remained a regular attraction at the Park for almost a decade, until concessionaires began complaining that patrons spent too much time at the circus and not enough in the Park. These complaints—in addition to the fact that the circus, which was set up in the parking lot, took away spaces for cars—led to the end of the big top at Palisades Park.

The end of the 1950s marked the death of Jack Rosenthal. Prior to his illness, Jack could frequently be heard on the midways of Palisades, playing one of his Stradivarius violins in his office. But Parkinson's disease eventually took its toll—although the colorful bachelor retained a healthy fondness for women up to the end. He took great pride in strolling through the Park with a woman on each arm, and rumor had it that he would lavish his ladies with mink coats and Cadillacs. When he finally succumbed to the disease, he was laid to rest in the band uniform that he had worn as concert master of the Cincinnati Symphony.

Irving inherited Jack's precious Stradivarius violin collection, and he became sole owner of the Park. By this time he was one of the nation's premier showmen, far removed from the poor adolescent who once sold pails and shovels on Coney Island's beaches. He

Jack Rosenthal (*The Palisadian*)

Irving Rosenthal (Bob Nesoff)

gave tours of the Park with the easy affability of a successful man showing off his estate. He reveled in the fact that a new generation of fun-seekers were filling his Park in record numbers. During the Memorial Day weekend of 1959, for example, the Park accommodated 260,000 patrons, sold 250,000 hot dogs and 40,000 gallons of lemonade, and returned 73 lost children to their parents.

In many ways Palisades had become Irving's home, and he lavished it with attention. He tasted all of his vendors' offerings, from the English-style french fries, steeped in salt and vinegar, to the mouth-watering roast beef sandwiches, and he always paid for whatever he ate. Before each day's opening he conducted white-glove inspections of every food and beverage stand (his philosophy was, "If a kid goes home with a sick stomach, we've lost a customer for life"). He became well known for his fetish of walking the midway streets and picking up refuse, and stories abounded of how he would delay an opening if he saw garbage on the ground, a broken light bulb, or a slip-shod paint job.

Irving, alone at the helm, prepared to guide Palisades into a new decade, and his unyielding devotion would drive the Park to new heights.

Above. Sleigh Ride (The Corbett Collection)

Right. Advertisement for Palisades Park, circa 1909 (Palisades Amusement Park Historical Society)

Below. Families come to the Park for a leisurely Sunday stroll (Author's Collection)

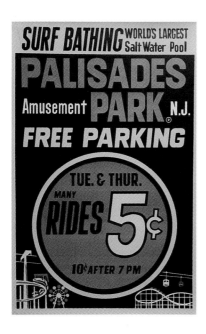

Above. Comic book coupons for Palisades Park
(National Periodicals)

Below. The Love Bugs ride (Peter Prinz)

Above. Poster ads for Palisades
Park (Author's Collection)

Right. The World's Largest Outdoor
Salt Water Pool (Peter Prinz)

Left. Main gate of the Park (P. J. Shelley/CPHS yearbook)

Center, left. Showboat Fun House in winter (Cliffside Park Free Public Library)

Center, right. Cyclone coaster (Peter Prinz)

Below. High above Palisades Amusement Park (Peter Prinz)

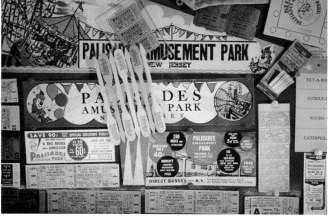

Above, right. The carousel lives on at Canada's Wonderland (E. Michael Sweeney)

Above, left. Memorabilia at Memories Restaurant (Memories Restaurant)

Right. Ticket booth for the Cyclone coaster outside Memories Restaurant (Fred Morrone)

The Later Years
1960-1971

*T*HE 1960s were, by all measures, the first decade in which business catered to adolescents—the sheer number of which few merchants could ignore. The Baby Boomers had money to spend, and many of them spent their money at Palisades. Palisades Amusement Park was *the* place to go. For many youngsters, the Park on the Palisades had become the super park.

Irving Rosenthal encouraged this perception through widespread publicity. Throughout the metropolitan area, posters and billboards invited patrons to "come on over." Palisades Amusement Park literally became a household word. This was particularly true after the famous Palisades jingle—written by Rosenthal's wife, songwriter Gladys Shelley—flooded the airwaves. Sung by Steve Clayton, a singer Shelley had used several years earlier to record her song "The Man with Seven Loves," and recorded at Capitol Recording Studios in New York, the jingle captured the spirit of the times:

> *Palisades has the rides,*
> *Palisades has the fun.*
> *Come on over.*
> *Shows and dancing are free,*
> *So's the parking, so, gee,*
> *Come on over.*
> *Palisades from coast to coast*
> *Where a dime buys the most,*

Palisades Amusement Park
Swings all day and after dark.
Ride the coaster, get cool
In the waves in the pool.
You'll have fun so come on over.

"We recorded it in twenty minutes, and little did I know at the time that it would run on radio and TV for well over eleven years," said Clayton, who remembered Palisades from his youth as the place that "brought a smile to everyone's face." The success of "Come on Over" boosted Clayton's popularity to new heights, and his voice was used to promote scores of other products, including Kool and Winston cigarettes, Reingold and Schaefer beer, Campbell's tomato soup, and Eastern Airlines. Each year, the song ushered in the beginning of spring. When radios reverberated with the strains of "Come on Over," it was a sure bet that warm weather was here to stay and a new season at the Park was beginning.

The advertising for the Park was both ingenious and ingenuous. Matchbooks prominently featured Palisades ads, each one guaranteeing free admission if it were presented at the gate. Those patrons lucky enough to find the face of a small boy—Pal, the Park's mascot—under the flap would also receive tickets for two free rides. And children eagerly purchased their favorite comics, knowing Palisades Amusement Park discount coupons and free admission passes were on the back pages.

Not surprisingly, the Park's association with comic book characters grew during this period. In a deal with DC Comics, Rosenthal

Sheet music for another Shelley song, "Color It Palisades Amusement Park" (Memories Restaurant)

arranged for America's favorite superhero, Superman, to become the Park's official spokesman. (The deal was undoubtedly helped by the fact that Rosenthal owned stock in DC's parent company, National Periodical Publications.) The Man of Steel appeared on billboards, posters, and the sides of buses, offering his personal invitation to visit the Park. (The Superman campaign proved so successful that the Park later introduced several Batman attractions, thanks to the popularity of the hit television show during the late sixties.)

The Park also struck deals with other comic-book publishers. In an agreement with Archie Comics, Palisades renamed its hot-rod ride Archie's Hot Rods. Harvey Comics contributed its famed TV and comic-book character, Casper the Friendly Ghost, to a redesign of the old Tunnel of Love. Over the years, the ride had replaced its boats with chariot-style cars that traveled along a track rather than a waterway. But the popularity of the automobile killed the tunnel's attraction as a place where young lovers could caress and kiss under cloak of darkness. The ride was redesigned with an Arabian Nights theme, but patrons were still uninterested. So now the Park turned to younger riders. The attraction was renamed Casper's Ghostland, and its dark caverns became populated by such Harvey Comic characters as Casper, the Villainous Ghostly Trio, Spooky the Tuff Little

Below, left. Matchbooks (Palisades Amusement Park Historical Society)

Below, right. Special discount ticket (Palisades Amusement Park Historical Society)

Bottom, right. Kiddieland ride ticket (front and back) (Palisades Amusement Park Historical Society)

Palisades Amusement Park

•

Top, left. Bumper cars (Cliffside Park Free Public Library)

Top, right. Soakyland and the Gold Spike Railroad (John and Margaret Winkler)

Above, left and right. The old Arabian Nights Tunnel of Love was renamed Caspar's Ghostland, after the Harvey Comics' character. (John and Margaret Winkler; Cliffside Park Free Public Library)

Ghost, and Nightmare the Ghost Horse. It became an overnight success. Harvey later donated their Wendy the Witch character to the Flying Teacups ride (which became Wendy's Cups and Saucers.) Both Archie and Harvey comics featured Palisades as the setting in various comic books.

As the decade progressed, promotional tie-ins became more and more commonplace at Palisades. When the Park offered free bags of groceries to the first thousand patrons who bought a book of discount combination tickets, eighteen of the top national grocery companies—including Proctor and Gamble, Hormel, General Foods,

The Park at night seen from Manhattan (Tom Meyers)

Quaker, and Hostess—gave away full-size boxes, cans, and bottles of such popular items as Top Job, Spam, Maxwell House coffee, Hi-C fruit drink, and Cap'n Crunch cereal. Ken-L-Ration sponsored the Big Little Dog Show. Mountain Dew backed the Country Music Talent Contest. And the rides might as well have been billboards; they included the Top Job Sky Ride, the Clark Gum Cyclone, the Cosmetically Yours Carousel, and the Hostess Cakes Trip to the Moon. (This last ride had originally been named the Astro Jet, until a letter from American Airlines informed the Park that the name was a registered trademark and could not be used on an amusement. Ironically, when a public relations man from American later visited the Park, he saw the huge letters spelling out "Hostess" on the rocket ship and asked how his airline could get its own name on a ride.)

By this time the moving sign on the cliffs had become integral in the Park's dynamic new wave of promotion. (It also provided a constant source of revenue; ads, sold by the week in blocks of one hundred characters, brought in an estimated two million dollars annually.) The Park traded-off advertising with area radio stations such as WINS, WMCA, and WNEW. It offered to put someone's name in lights as a prize on a national television show. It even used the sign for personal messages; when a popular DJ in the fifties and sixties, Jack Eigin, was fired from his radio station job, the sign read, "Keep your chin up, Jack. Tomorrow's a better day." (A despondent Eigin saw the message while driving on the West Side Highway in New York, and he later said it gave him the lift he needed.) The sign

A turn-of-the-century high-diving bicyclist (John and Margaret Winkler)

was run year-round, and changing the sign's message required a long, dangerous climb up a ladder to a small booth high above the cliffs.

Through any means available, Rosenthal kept the Park in the limelight—even if it called for occasional chicanery. In 1964, for instance, Palisades consistently recorded better attendance figures than the rival World's Fair, which was being held that summer in New York. The reason was simple, as Sol Abrams remembered: "We would call up the management of the World's Fair and say we were the *Hudson Dispatch* newspaper and needed to know that day's attendance figures. They would look up their gate receipts and tell them to me. After I hung up, I'd add thirty thousand to their total and release that number to the press as our attendance."

And through it all, the crowds kept coming to Palisades Park.

PALISADES still offered many novelty acts that added a certain circus-like atmosphere to the Park. These included balloonists, parachute jumpers, motorcycle-riding lions, pole sitters, human cannon-

★ ★

The Charitable Side of Irving Rosenthal

Irving Rosenthal has been described a strict man, a demanding man, a perfectionist, and he certainly had a salty vocabulary. He commanded attention and respect from everyone he met. And though he may have been a man small of stature—he stood barely five feet tall—he had the heart of a giant. When a movie or television company wanted to use the Park, the fee was donated directly to Rosenthal's pet charity, the New York Association for Brain Injured Children in Kerhonkson, New York. He would also annually open the gates of his Park for the New York Police Anchor Club; more than seventy-five hundred orphaned and

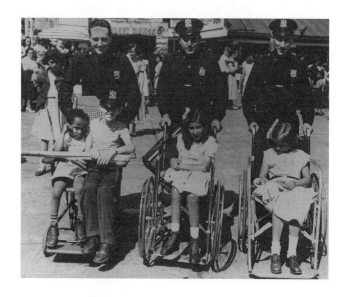

Above, left. New York Police Anchor Club (Cliffside Park Free Public Library)

Above, right. Three policeman escorting children at the annual Police Anchor Club outing (*The Record*)

Left. Policeman tumbles with children inside the Barrel of Fun in the fun house, 1953 (*The Record*)

Palisades Amusement Park
•

Above, left. Irving Rosenthal (Bob Nesoff)

Above, right. Rosenthal and youngster with scale-model of the Park (Memories Restaurant)

handicapped children of every race, color, and creed were bused to the Park by off-duty police officers and given free tickets for rides and food. This event, begun in 1937, continued every year thereafter.

Irving Rosenthal demonstrated his love for children in other ways as well. He would approach children randomly on the midways and ask if they could sing the Palisades Park jingle. If they did, he'd give them a dollar. He also gave kids a dollar if they called him Uncle Irving. Once, a DJ who had heard about this story broadcast it over the New York airwaves. That weekend Rosenthal was deluged with kids who wanted to say hello to their newest "uncle." It cost him about one thousand dollars.

However, Rosenthal also knew how to combine his love of children with good business sense. In the back of the Park, just behind the free-act stage, was a hole in the fence. Local children knew about this hole and used it to sneak into the Park without paying the admission fee. What the children didn't know was that Rosenthal also knew about the hole, and he had instructed the Park's security guards to turn their backs if they saw any kids sneaking in. Rosenthal believed that children would spend all their dollars once inside the Park, but they might not come in at all if there were an admission fee. So hundreds of local boys and girls thought they were putting something over on Uncle Irving, who just kept on smiling and looked the other way.

★ ★

balls, diving horses, music-playing leopards, illusionists, jugglers, acrobats, and high-wire daredevils.

And interspersed among the rides and food concessions were numerous games of skill inviting visitors to throw softballs at fuzzy stuffed cats, pitch coins onto slippery dishes, or attempt some other feat. These games offered every prize imaginable, including candy, ham, bacon, toys, bathroom scales, small appliances, dolls, clocks, and cigarettes. Live pets offered the most thrilling prizes for youngsters, especially parakeets (even though they had acquired the nickname "Japanese Keelers" for chirping once and then keeling over). And there's probably many a Bergen County Baby Boomer who still has one of those tiny, round fish bowls—once filled with colored water and a single goldfish—stashed somewhere in the attic. The prize was won by landing a ping-pong ball inside the narrow opening of the fish bowl. (Many of the unwanted fish were dumped in the murky waters of a Park boat ride, Jungleland; by the end of the season, the fish had grown into huge carp that were then caught by Rosenthal's chauffeur, Leon Robinson, and taken home as dinner.)

Then there were the beauty pageants. During the 1960s, Palisades Amusement Park became the beauty pageant capital of the world. The contests, many of them televised, were annual events that developed their own following. At any one time, there could be fifteen or more queens in attendance at the Park—enough for any Royal Ball.

September 1960 marked the debut of the Miss American Teen-Ager Pageant. The contest, open to girls between the ages of thirteen and seventeen, was filmed for TV at the Park's Casino restaurant, with the massive saltwater pool used as a backdrop. The finalists waited on the east side of the pool, and as their names were announced they were brought over to the Casino by paddleboat. This contest proved popular through the years and attracted many talented contestants; by 1964, over thirty-five thousand young women were participating. In the later years, the winner's rewards included an all-expense-paid, round-trip flight to Hollywood; the opportunity to audition for television roles in *The Courtship of Eddie's Father*, *Nanny and the Professor*, and *General Hospital*; a new Dodge Challenger; a Florida vacation; a $1,000 wardrobe; a diamond watch; the complete twenty-four-volume set of the 1971 Encyclopedia Britannica; a pedigree poodle; an eight-track stereo; and a one-year scholarship to the New York Academy of Theatrical Arts.

One of the most popular pageants, Little Miss America, debuted in 1961. Girls between the ages of five and ten were judged on the

★ ★

A Partial List of Competitions at Palisades

A.A.U. Hudson County Annual Swim Meet (1915)

Baby Parade (1908)

Baby Show (1908)

Baby Walking Race

Beautiful Legs Contest (1945)

Big Little Dog Contest

Charleston Contest (1925)

Country Music Talent Search

Diaper Derby (1938)

Eyeglass-wearing Beauty Contest (1941)

Fall Festival Queen

Healthiest Child Contest (1937)

Little Miss America

Miss American Secretary

Miss American Starlet

Miss American Teen-Ager

Miss American Vampire

Miss Fat America

Miss German America

Miss Hot Pants

Miss Italian America

Miss Latin America

Miss Palisades Amusement Park (1925)

Miss Polish America

Miss Universe sectionals

Most Photographic Triplets (1947)

Most Photographic Triplets and Twins

Mrs. America (1939)

Mrs. Grandmother

New Jersey State Donut Dunking Championship (1940)

N.J.A.A.U. Championship Swimming Carnival (1936)

New Jersey State Dancing Championship (1927)

New Jersey State Tango Dancing Championship (1927)

Outdoor Fun Queen

P.A.P. Dance Contest

P.A.P. Photography Contest (1941)

Palisades Poster Girl

Queen of Golden Jubilee

Shoe Shine Contest

Miss American Secretary (Memories Restaurant)

Spaghetti-eating Contest

Stubble Trouble Contest (fastest shaver; 1946)

Sweater Queen

Tall Beauty

Valley Fair Step to Stardom

Venida Hair Queen Contest (1945)

★ ★

basis of beauty, charm, poise, and personality. These productions attracted thousands of stage mothers from every corner of the country to drag their little beauties to Palisades. Six thousand girls came each week to compete; add to this the mothers, fathers, grandparents, aunts, and uncles who came to watch, and it's not surprising that long lines of patrons would wind around the Park. Not everyone appreciated the contest, however; the Atlantic City-based Miss America Pageant sued Palisades—unsuccessfully—for using the name Little Miss America.

One of the most prominent people in the production of these pageants was Jan LeWinter. Jan ran a dance studio, and she was selected to produce the pageants for seven years, from 1964 to 1971. She hosted Little Miss America, Miss American Teen-Ager, and The

Bus poster for Miss American Teen-Ager contest (P. J. Shelley/CPHS yearbook)

New Talent Showcase. One of Jan's students was a seven-year-old girl who loved to sing. During the contests, while the judges deliberated, she sang *a cappella* to entertain the crowd. The child grew up to be the Academy Award–winning Irene Cara from the movie *Fame*.

Judges for the pageants included notables such as comedian Jack Carter, the *Little Rascals'* Darla Hood, and comedian Joey Adams (who met his wife, Cindy, while she was a contestant in one of the pageants). The pageants became so popular at Palisades that a sign was temporarily placed by one of the entrances that read, "Through these portals pass the most beautiful girls in the world!" There were pageants of all types, including several that celebrated the ethnicity of American society: Miss Polish American, Miss Italian American, Miss German American, and Mrs. Latin American (later changed to *Miss* Latin American because many Hispanic men did not want their wives to compete). Other titles included Miss Hot Pants, Mrs. America, Miss Fat America, World's Best-Looking Grandmother, Tall Beauty, Fall Festival Queen, Teen Queen, Beautiful Legs, Sweater Queen, Outdoor Fun Queen, Miss American Secretary, and Miss American Vampire. (The crown and scepter were recycled for each pageant; only the sash with the queen's title changed.) "You name the contest and we have the Queen!" Sol Abrams was often heard to remark. It was hard to argue with him.

The contests at Palisades didn't always involve beauty, though. The Park featured new talent with events such as the New Talent Showcase, the Valley Fair Step to Stardom, and the Miss American Starlet pageant, which gave away trips to Hollywood. The Country Music Talent Contest awarded each winner a recording contract with Audio Fidelity Records and a new guitar, among other prizes. Infants could wriggle along the sixty-foot course of the Diaper Derby, the only Park event in which contestants would sometimes fail to leave the starting line because they had fallen asleep. (In July 1964, a new record time was set at sixty-one seconds. The winner received a $25 savings bond.) And, through Ken-L-Ration's Big Little

Above, left. Little Miss America semi-finals (Margaret M. Wylie)

Above, right. Little Miss America on her throne (*The Record*)

Left. The new Little Miss America (Cliffside Park Free Public Library)

Below. Little Miss America pageant (Cliffside Park Free Public Library)

The Later Years, 1960–1971

Above, left. First prize winner of Baby and Carriage contest, circa 1908 (*The Palisadian*)

Above, right. The Triplets Convention (*The Record*)

Left. The winner of the 1943 Diaper Derby (*The Palisadian*)

Dog Show, canines could compete for such titles as Best Costumed Dog, Dog with the Best Tricks, and Dog Hero of the Year.

The Park also held a Twins Convention and a popular Triplets Convention. One year, it featured the eighty-eight-year-old triplets Faith, Hope, and Charity. That day at Palisades, the trio of octogenarians took their first ride on a carousel in seventy-five years.

The contests provided Palisades with a great deal of publicity during this decade, and they attracted substantial crowds. Yet, as popular as these event were, many Baby Boomers best remember Palisade for its music—specifically, rock 'n' roll.

Music had always been a solid part of the Park's drawing power. From its first days, the Park showcased the changing musical tastes of America. Its shows were so popular that over the years many of them were broadcast live on radio and TV. As early as 1924, WHN-AM in New York carried the Charles Strickland Orchestra over its

Top. The Diaper Derby contestants at the starting gate, 1953 (*The Record*)

Above, left. Best Decorated Baby Carriage (*The Palisadian*)

Above, right. The annual Diaper Derby (Cliffside Park Free Public Library)

airwaves, and by 1925 the station was broadcasting a bi-weekly program of Strickland's dance music that was hosted by the "Voice of the Great White Way," Nils T. Granlun. In 1926, WPAP-AM, the Park's own resident radio station, began broadcasting the music.

However, the arrival of rock 'n' roll heralded a new era. This exciting, contagious sound would break every record that ever stood in the music world, and Palisades Amusement Park—already drawing large crowds of teenagers in the very influential New York City media market—rode the crest of its popularity.

Many consider Bill Silbert, a Park DJ during the early 1950s, the father of the pop music era at Palisades. Every Saturday around 5:00 p.m., Silbert hosted a live, one-hour dance show that featured the talents of pop artists such as Tony Bennett, Eddie Fisher, Vic Damone, Eileen Barton, and Mel Torme. The shows were televised on New York's Channel 5, and Silbert came to command such respect that Eddie Fisher offered him a part in a movie in which he and Debbie Reynolds were starring. (Silbert accepted and used the screen name of Bill Blake.)

When the Park introduced batting cages, it brought in Murray Kaufman, who was a catcher with the New York Yankees farm team, to help with publicity. When he saw Bill Silbert host the dance show, Kaufman said to himself, "I can do that," and convinced Rosenthal into giving him a shot at the music shows.

Kaufman—later known as Murray the K—and Silbert hosted the shows simultaneously. The personalities of the two men were quite different—Silbert preferred the light, contemporary sounds while Kaufman remained on the cutting edge of rock 'n' roll. Over time, Murray the K began bringing in more of his rock 'n' roll bands, which led to a new era of music at the Park.

Near the end of the "Fabulous Fifties," a new name was added to the list of Palisades Amusement Park personalities, Cousin Bruce Morrow. Morrow—a swinging, super-cool DJ—began hosting a weekly Battle of the Bands, introducing fine new talent to the Park's audiences. He also hosted the Park's Top 40 shows, broadcast weekly from a special glass-enclosed radio studio built within the Casino restaurant. His program (first broadcast on WINS radio, then WABC) soared to such heights that he was able to attract many of the hottest names in show business. Bobby Rydell, Frankie Avalon, Fabian, Bill Haley and the Comets, the Shirelles, Little Anthony, the Shangri-Las, the Rascals, the Lovin' Spoonful, and Petula Clark all appeared on the Park's stage, as did New Jersey native Lesley Gore—"the Cutie Pie from Tenafly"—who introduced many of her hits there. (Once, while performing her hit song "It's My Party," Gore caught her heel in a small hole on the old wooden stage. She performed the entire song without moving her left foot. At the conclusion of the song, Cousin Brucie joined her on stage. She stepped out of her shoe and Morrow picked it up, while the understanding crowd at Palisades cheered her performance.)

Another host joining Palisades' roster of talent was Clay Cole.

Above. The open-air stage (Cliffside Park Free Public Library)

Right. Five musicians on stage overlooking crowd and the Flight to Mars (*The Record*/Ed Hill)

Below. Cousin Brucie walks out on stage in his leopardskin suit (Ed Hill)

The Later Years, 1960–1971
•
97

He broadcast a weekly television show called "Rock 'n' Roll Show—Live from Palisades Park." A frequent guest on his TV show was Cousin Brucie, and Cole often repaid the favor by appearing on Brucie's radio show. Irving Rosenthal encouraged this swapping of personalities to cross-promote his amusement park.

None of the musical acts that performed at Palisades was ever paid; instead the acts received promotion, which meant increased record sales from the adoring fans. Irving frequently reminded Cousin Brucie that the acts would receive "a million dollars' worth of publicity." In these early days of television, lip syncing was generally accepted and especially so at Palisades Park. Almost every performer lip synced his or her songs, saving both the time and the money incurred by bringing in live musicians. Usually the performances went without mishap, but not always. Once, Tony Bennett refused to lip sync his chart-topping "I Left My Heart in San Francisco," and only the insistent coaxing of Cousin Brucie persuaded him to relent. Then, halfway through Bennett's performance, the ultimate indignity happened: the record began to skip. Cousin Brucie had to return to the stage to bail out the embarrassed singer. The most likely cause for the misfortune was the condition of the Park's antiquated sound system. Morrow would later recall, "The equipment probably came from Civil War days. It was just awful. The turntable and the stylus were like a claw and a hammer." Fortunately, the Palisades audience overlooked the *faux pas*.

Throughout the decade, music played a crucial role at Palisades. In addition to its pop and rock 'n' roll acts, the Park broadcast folk singers and comedians from the Village's Bitter End club, including stars such as Phil Ochs, José Feliciano, and Bill Cosby. Pepsi Cola sponsored a weekly country music show at Palisades starring Smokey Warren—the "Eastern King of Western Swing"—and his Arizona Trail Blazers. (The name of Warren's band later changed to the Mountain Dew Boys, after a new soft drink brought out by Pepsi.) The show's guests included Tex Ritter, Johnny Paycheck, Eddie Rabbit, and other stars from the Grand Ole Opry. Even Polka Dance Parties with the renowned Jimmy Sturr, Eddie Granite, Johnny Budd, and Dick Pillar found their way onto the Palisades venue.

Yet nothing approached the popularity of Cousin Brucie's rock 'n' roll shows; the Park even took out a contract with Lloyds of London to guarantee a performance by Fabian. These shows, however, proved a mixed blessing to Irving Rosenthal. Rosenthal loved the fact that they drew large crowds, but their length often kept the audiences from roaming through the Park and spending money. (He

Tony Bennett and Cousin Brucie (Ed Hill)

would frequently be heard screaming to Morrow, "Brucie, you're killing me!")

Around 1964, Murray the K left Palisades to work for a nearby competitor, Freedomland. Morrow took over the position formerly held by Murray the K and began booking the shows as well as hosting them. But with radio stations still recovering from the payola scandals of the late fifties, it looked bad to have a deejay booking acts for a venue as large as the Palisades. Irving and Cousin Brucie decided it would be safer to let an outside agent book the acts. The Park initially turned over the job to Bob Austin, the publisher of a popular record magazine. Austin soon quit, and the Park—recognizing that the airwaves were now filled with the sounds of rhythm and blues—turned to the top black disk jockey of the day, Hal Jackson. Jackson, a thirty-year veteran in radio and television, knew many of

Hal Jackson with The Fifth Dimension (Cliffside Park Free Public Library)

the country's top soul talent and had even been credited with giving some of the performers their first breaks; more than a decade earlier he had introduced audiences in Washington, D.C., to Sammy Davis, Jr. His other accomplishments included introducing rock 'n' roll to Carnegie Hall and, with Eleanor Roosevelt, broadcasting the complete American tour of the Emperor Haile Selassie.

Jackson broadcast daily from the Park between 1:00 and 6:00 p.m. over WNJR, playing fresh R & B sounds and attracting top stars such as the Jackson Five, Diana Ross and the Supremes, the Temptations, and the Fifth Dimension. Eventually, his shows were also televised from Palisades. Together, Jackson and Morrow made Palisades synonymous with rock 'n' roll to an entire generation of young people.

By the mid-1960s the Park was more popular than ever. Its TV commercials usually appeared between the hours of 3:00 and 6:00 p.m., when children were arriving home from school. These youngsters could not get through twenty-seven minutes of the *Three Stooges* or *Huckleberry Hound* without at least five Palisades Amusement Park advertisements.

One time Sonny Fox, host of the popular children's television show *Wonderama*, made an appearance at Palisades on a brutally hot day. Hundreds of children showed up to see their favorite star. Palisades, which had not counted on Fox's popularity, had little security for the event—only one officer named Warren was assigned to control the crowd.

★ ★

Palisades Park Hits the Music Charts

One day in the early 1960s, a young employee of ABC television was driving along New York's Riverside Drive when he glanced across the Hudson at the glimmering amusement park high on the Palisades cliffs. He began humming a tune, then added lyrics that he felt captured the Park's spirit. He kept adding lyrics over the next several weeks, until finally one night he sat down with his Martin six-string guitar and recorded the melody onto a tape (he couldn't read or write music). The man's name was Chuck Barris, and he titled his song "Amusement Park."

Barris mailed copies of the song to two of his rock 'n' roll idols, Bobby Rydell and Freddy "Boom Boom" Cannon. Cannon, known for such hits as "Tallahassee Lassie" and "Way Down Yonder in New Orleans," agreed to put it on the B-side of his upcoming record, "June, July, and August." After some consideration, Cannon and Barris decided to rename the song "Palisades Park."

When Irving Rosenthal heard it, he naturally fell in love with it—what more fitting tribute to his Park than a rock 'n' roll song that would appeal to the young people he loved so much? Irving asked Bruce Morrow to play it on his nighttime radio program. Morrow did so, and in less than two weeks the song was among the top ten nationwide. The song rose to number three on the charts for two weeks in 1962 and remained for fifteen weeks among the best sellers. By the end of the summer, the record had sold two million copies—a quarter of a million in the New York tri-state area alone; special shipments of the record had to be trucked in on Saturday mornings to accommodate the demand. The song even achieved international recognition when it climbed to the number twenty position in Britain, remaining eight weeks among the best sellers. The A-side of the record never came close to the popularity of "Palisades Park," as people across the country and across the Atlantic chanted the words that Barris had created.

> *You'll never know how great a kiss could feel,*
> *When you're stuck at the top of a Ferris wheel*
> *Where I fell in love . . . down at Palisades Park.*

The odds of an unknown songwriter achieving a nationwide hit were slim, and the song's success immediately put Barris under suspicion. He was summoned into the office of the ABC chief counsel, who had assumed that Barris had used his position at the network—as well as payoffs—to get music programmers to play his song. Barris assured the counsel that no wrongdoing had taken place. After much persuasion, he was permitted to stay—provided he sign a letter stating he would never write another song as long as he worked at the American Broadcasting Company. Barris agreed, but over the next five years he continued writing songs under pseudonyms. Several of them did well, but none were as big as "Palisades Park," and Barris eventually went on to achieve fame as the producer of such top-rated television game shows as *The Newlywed Game*, *The Dating Game*, and *The Gong Show*.

★ ★

Warren, not accustomed to the fracas that was occurring, began pushing back the children as they scrambled to get close to the TV host. Fox said to Warren that he would take care of the kids, and asked him not to be so rough. But Warren continued pushing and yelling at the youngsters. Finally Fox demanded Warren's badge number. Warren refused. When Fox reached to see the number on the badge, Warren declared, "You are under arrest for assaulting a police officer."

Although being arrested was far from why Fox had come to the Park, he thought this was his ticket to immortality—a children's television star arrested for defending the youngsters he loved so dearly. The headlines would guarantee that Fox's name would be permanently remembered.

Fox finished his appearance and signed every photo. After that, Warren escorted him back to the administration building. When they arrived, Irving Rosenthal demanded to know what this was all about. Warren informed the Park owner that Fox was being arrested because he interfered with a police officer in the line of duty. Irving became furious. He screamed at the policeman, "How dare you arrest this man! He came here as a guest of the Park!" Irving then informed Warren that he was fired and would never work at Palisades Amusement Park again.

Many of the popular television shows of the day used the Park as a colorful backdrop. Bozo the Clown celebrated his ten-year anniversary on New York television at the Park's outdoor stage. *The Today Show* with Dave Garroway broadcast a week's worth of their shows from the Park. Soupy Sales filmed a series of *Philo Kvetch* episodes at the Park, and *Reingold Playhouse* did the same with its show *The Fun Master* starring Keenan Wynn. *Man Against Crime* with Ralph Bellamy filmed some spectacular footage from the Cyclone roller coaster, and NBC's *Wide Wide World* made television history when it bolted a live camera onto the front car of the coaster. Goodson and Todman's *What's My Line* show would often ask the Park to send over someone with an oddball occupation, such as the man who "Blows Women's Skirts Up" in the fun house or a "Cotton Candy Maker."

The producers once asked Abrams to supply a guest for their popular game show, *To Tell the Truth*. It was decided that Pat Jamison, the wild-animal trainer at the circus, would be perfect. The events that followed were less so.

On the day of the show, Jamison went into Manhattan with a cheetah attached to a huge chain. She was accompanied by Abrams and the cheetah's owner, John Cuneo. Their first stop was a press

Midways in the sixties (Cliffside Park Free Public Library)

conference at a Fifty-seventh Street hotel. When they arrived, however, the cheetah saw its reflection in a store window and, startled, ran down the street, dragging Jamison behind. The trainer eventually got the animal under control, and they proceeded to meet the press.

The trio—plus cheetah—arrived at the Goodson and Todman studios around noon. Outside the building, several women on their lunch breaks were sunning themselves around a fountain. When the cheetah saw the water, it immediately ran for a drink, and the frightened women tumbled backwards with a splash. Cuneo quickly retrieved the cheetah, and they hastily entered the building.

When the elevator arrived, Pat, Sol, and the cheetah boarded the elevator. Before John could get in, though, the door closed on the chain and the elevator rose. The choke collar tightened and began to strangle the helpless cheetah, who hissed and growled until the chain snapped. After several frightening minutes, the car returned to the ground floor and John threw his coat over the crazed, panting animal. The cheetah eventually calmed down, and the episode of *To Tell the Truth* was finally taped.

Another time, the producers of the newly popular television show *Sesame Street* came to visit the Park. Rosenthal took one of the producers, a black woman, to the edge of the pool and demonstrated the water's clarity by dropping a dime to the bottom, twelve feet down. The woman looked at him and said, "Mr. Rosenthal, I know your pool very well. When I was a teenager, I was one of the

At Palisades Amusement Park, Bozo the Clown celebrates his tenth successful year with WPIX-TV (© 1994 Larry Harmon Pictures Corp. All rights reserved.)

persons on the picket line." Times had definitely changed.

Television wasn't the only medium with which Palisades Amusement Park became associated. In the fifties, Palisades had been seen in the motion pictures *The World, the Flesh, and the Devil* and *Somebody Up There Likes Me*, which had starred Paul Newman. In 1961 Sol Abrams convinced the producers of the musical *West Side Story* to plaster posters for the Park in several of the movie's most important scenes. A few years later, the Park showcased the Astin Martin from the 1964 James Bond film, *Goldfinger*. The attraction, with an admission price of twenty-five cents, grossed ten thousand dollars for the Park. Palisades had acquired the car with the help of Jay Emmett, who had started the Licensing Corporation of America at the suggestion of Irving Rosenthal. Emmett, who would eventually become president of Warner Brothers, later helped the Park install the 007 Shooting Gallery.

Not all of the changes at the Park were happy ones during this decade. On June 22, 1962, the Park's superintendent of almost thirty years, Joe McKee, died. During his tenure, Palisades became a magnet for roller-coaster aficionados. Thanks to their location at the top of a two-hundred-foot cliff, the Park's coasters offered the illusion

Roller Coaster Fans

Roller coasters have developed such a following that several organizations have been formed by their fans. A.C.E. (American Coaster Enthusiasts), one of the largest such associations, regularly plans outings to America's finest parks to experience the thrills of their coasters.

Today's coasters are faster and more thrilling than ever before. We've come a long way since the days of the "Death Swing" when the daredevil made an upside down loop while the crowd watched. Now the patrons demand loops and twists and turns that years ago were relegated to the hired performers. Today there are many fine coasters throughout the country. At Cedar Point in Sandusky, Ohio, stands the nation's tallest wooden coaster "The Mean Streak." It rises over one hundred and sixty-one feet into the air.

that they were the highest in the world—when cars paused at the crest of that first steep incline, all of New York City lay at the riders' feet. Joe McKee had greatly helped to enhance that reputation. In addition to the Cyclone, he had built the Giant Coaster, a smaller version of the Cyclone for those not brave enough to ride his monstrous masterpiece, and the Wild Mouse, a wooden coaster in which two-passenger cars, their wheels fixed to the center of the chassis, gave the illusion they were about to go over the edge of sharp ess turns. McKee had been a legendary figure, and his loss was felt around the globe.

His replacement was a mechanical wizard by the name of Joe Rinaldi. Like his predecessor, Rinaldi excelled in designing safety devices for the rides; one of his most notable was a special cowling that kept long hair from becoming tangled around the pivoting axis of the Ferris wheel.

Then on July 16, 1963, a quarter of a million dollars worth of laughs went up in smoke when the fun house was gutted by flames. The fire broke out after the Park had closed, at about 12:20 a.m. Fifteen pieces of fire fighting equipment battled the blaze, which took about an hour to bring under control. (One fireman commented on the difficulty of fighting the flames in the fun house's tilted room.) It was believed that the fire had started as the result of a short circuit.

Irving Rosenthal announced that a portable fun house would be imported from Hamburg, Germany, until the permanent one could be rebuilt. Within a week, Cleopatra's Barge, as it was called, stood in front of the charred remains of the old fun house. Its front facade spanned the width of the old building. Press releases touted the ride as an unforgettable experience. Upon paying the admission price,

Above and below. The Wild Mouse (Peter Prinz; P. J. Shelley/CPHS yearbook)

Left. Joe Rinaldi (The Rinaldi Family)

Palisades Amusement Park

•

★ ★

Controlling Crowds through Colors

In the mid-1960s, the Park received a new look. Jack Ray, an expert on colors in amusement parks, changed the Park's red, white, and blue motif to various shades of greens, oranges, and yellows (known as mezzotint), which he then systematically used to control crowds. Bright, friendly colors such as pink, yellow, or orange drew large numbers of patrons. Dark colors such as burgundy or brown had the opposite effect, subconsciously making people avoid a particular area. Sounds were used in a similar manner; loud, snappy pop music—especially songs with lyrics—always attracted throngs. The colors and sounds were arranged throughout the Park so that patrons had to pass the less-popular stands to reach their favorite attractions—allowing the slower stands to pick up business.

(Interestingly enough, the exact colors chosen were based on a dress owned by Mrs. Rosenthal, Gladys Shelley. "It was the most colorful dress you ever saw," recalled park superintendent John Rinaldi. "We adopted about ten colors from it.")

★ ★

however, patrons soon learned that the attraction offered them little more than a seat on a bench while walls decorated with Egyptian artifacts rotated around them—a feeble attempt at making them think they were spinning upside down. Cleopatra's Barge turned out to be a miserable dud, and it became clear that Joe Rinaldi would have to make the reconstruction of the fun house a top priority.

But in the fall of 1963 Joe Rinaldi also died, and Rosenthal decided to pass the job on to Rinaldi's son, John. John Rinaldi had worked at the Park as a consultant since the age of fifteen, planning and supervising programs for teenagers. Now, at the age of twenty-nine, he became the youngest general superintendent in the outdoor-amusement industry. It was said that, like Joe McKee and Rosenthal himself, he could walk past the Cyclone coaster and tell if there was anything wrong just by listening. Third in command, John answered only to Irving and Anna Cook, and he soon justified the confidence they placed in him.

Rinaldi immediately set about refurbishing the fun house. Along with Jack Ray, an expert on color arrangement, he came up with the Showboat Fun House. The facade of the new attraction resembled a Mississippi showboat, right down to the water cascading over its turning paddles. A quintet of moving mannequin musicians performed incessant Dixieland melodies, while on the top deck a cheerful captain stood firmly at the wheel. Inside, the attraction was replete with several of the celebrated features of the old fun house, such as the dark room, the revolving barrel, two air blowers (although the old fun house had many more blowers because more

Right. Painters at work on the Cockeyed Circus fun house, 1950 (*The Record*)

Below, left. Firemen gather outside of the Cockeyed Circus fun house, July 16, 1963. (*The Record*/Ed Hill)

Below, right. Firemen pour water inside the smoldering fun house. (*The Record*/Ed Hill)

Bottom, left. Conveyer belts take patrons on a wild ride. (Memories Restaurant)

Bottom, right. Fun house mirrors (Memories Restaurant)

Palisades Amusement Park

Left. Southeast corner of the Park (John and Margaret Winkler)

Below, left. Hal Jackson and Emily McDonald, the Park's switchboard operator, in front of the fun house (Cliffside Park Free Public Library)

Below, right. The Showboat Fun House (P. J. Shelley/CPHS yearbook)

Bottom, left. John Rinaldi and carousel operator John Winkler (John and Margaret Winkler)

Bottom, right. Model helps put the finishing touches on the Showboat fun house 1967. (*The Record*)

The Later Years, 1960–1971
•

John Rinaldi, Irving Rosenthal, Morgan Hughes, and Patty Conklin (Memories Restaurant)

women wore skirts back then), and the Magic Carpet, a collapsing bench that sent a patron on a bumpy journey down a conveyor belt. It also offered revolving disks, an obstacle course, shaker platforms, wrong-direction conveyor belts, and crazy mirrors. All told, the Showboat Fun House boasted thirty-five attractions for the price of one admission.

By this time, Mickey Hughes had become the largest importer of amusement park rides on the continent. His name became synonymous with foreign rides, and his association with Palisades would turn him into a millionaire. He traveled the globe so often that he maintained homes in several countries. In Canada, Morgan Hughes had Patty Conklin's Canadian National Exposition as his showcase. In Europe, the Oktoberfest in Munich served as Hughes's informal showcase for his rides.

Hughes had a keen sense for the industry he loved so much and he kept up with the changing trends. He saw the new use of fiberglass in the rides' construction and capitalized on the new craze for high-fidelity sound by bringing over rides featuring the finest French sound systems.

"The lighting and decorations are gorgeous over there [in Europe], they have such pride in their equipment," Hughes said at the time. "I don't think we [in this country] have the interest, generally, in the beauty of our equipment. . . . I've not had operators come over to me at Palisades and say, 'Mickey, the background, that painting—it's beautiful.' But in Germany they go over and admire the scenery and compliment the ride's owner. They actually congratulate him! That's one of the things I want to stimulate in this country: Admiration for the equipment."

The rides Hughes brought to Palisades included:

- **Sky Ride.** Stretching from one end of the Park to the other, the Sky Ride was added in 1964. (Hughes also installed the ride at Palisades' nearest competition that year, the World's Fair.) It offered a breathtaking, panoramic view of the Park and the Manhattan skyline.

- **Monorail.** The "transportation of the future" slowly wound its way in and around the midways of Palisades.

- **German Fun House (Hofbrauhaus).** Oktoberfest was the theme of this attraction. Upon entering, patrons found a rocking floor and beer barrels precariously stacked to the ceiling, looking as though they could tumble at any moment. After climbing a set of moving steps, patrons encountered a dark maze, a hall of mirrors, and other assorted amusements before finally exiting through a large Barrel of Fun.

- **Jet Star / Wild Cat.** Both of these steel coasters featured sharp banks and turns and dramatic vertical drops. The Wild Cat, not quite as fast as the Jet Star, measured 178 feet long by 65 feet high and boasted a triple spiral on each end.

- **Jungleland.** This boat trip down the murky rivers of "darkest Africa" featured moving crocodiles, rhinoceroses, hippos, gorillas, snakes, and more. (Jungleland was once used by a patron to dispose of an unwanted baby alligator, which wasn't discovered by Park officials until it had become fully grown.)

- **Himalaya / Super Himalaya.** Both Himalayas were circular rides with highback hills and humps; patrons were forced to the sides of the cars as the speed increased. The rides featured loud popular music played by a disk jockey/ride operator who spoke to the riders, asking if they wanted to go faster or perhaps travel backwards.

- **Disk Express / Flying Bobs.** In these rides, cars were suspended on bars from the center of a hub that rotated and forced the cars to become nearly perpendicular. Each car seated two patrons side by side and could travel both forwards and backwards to the beat of loud music. The Disk Express disappeared after an accident in the late sixties and came back redesigned as the Flying Bobs.

Above. The Sky Ride (Peter Prinz)

Left. Jungleland (Memories Restaurant)

Below. The German Fun House (Memories Restaurant)

Palisades Amusement Park

•

- **Swiss Bobs / Bayern Curve.** Ten bobsleds were connected in this ride, with each sled accommodating two riders. Patrons were propelled around a glistening winter landscape, encountering no dips and bumps, only shapely banked turns.

For the children, miniature versions of rides were offered in Kiddieland. An amusement park within the Park, Kiddieland featured a roller coaster, a Whip, and a carousel, as well as assorted buses, race cars, tanks, fire engines, boats, stagecoaches, and rocket ships. Larger-than-life cartoon characters and wooden soldiers stood tall among the rides, and the area was thoughtfully lined with seats and benches where mothers and fathers could rest.

By the late 1960s, the combination of rides, music, and contests had thousands pouring through the Palisades gates. Sooner or later everyone came to the Park, including celebrities such as Walter

★ ★

Employees through the Years

Over the years, thousands of people were employed at Palisades Amusement Park. They were the ones responsible for awakening the Park in the spring, letting it frolic on hot summer nights, and putting it to bed in the fall. They were as diverse as the many jobs they performed: professionals and amateurs, full time and part time, students and senior citizens.

For many a youngster, Palisades offered them their first jobs. A Park position was almost guaranteed if you lived in the area and had the desire to work. Cliffside Park Mayor Gerald Calabrese, a former soda jerk at the Park, recalled, "During the Depression, any kid in Cliffside Park could have gotten a job at the Park just for asking."

Senior citizens were hired mainly as ticket takers, gatekeepers, or concessionaires. These elder employees displayed a very special love for youngsters, treating them as though they were their own grandchildren. The Park recognized the knowledge, wisdom, dedication, and commitment of older workers, who instantly became part of the Palisades family and gave the Park the "mom and pop" atmosphere for which it became known.

Nepotism also became part of the character of Palisades. Fathers would pass their jobs on to sons, mothers would pass theirs onto daughters. When fourteen-year-old Linda Paulson started in the summer of '63, she represented 132 collective years of Paulsons working in the Park; her great-uncle had joined Palisades in 1911, and her grandfather came a year later.

Palisades' mix of seniors and young people allowed it to be open even while school was in session. The Park remained open from Easter Sunday through Labor Day (causing some season openings to be delayed due to snowstorms). It was one of the few parks in the country that could enjoy such a long season, since most amusement parks employed a majority of students and couldn't operate daily until June. At Palisades, senior citizens filled the void when student employees were in school.

★ ★

Below, left. Connie Francis (Memories Restaurant)

Below, right. Walter Cronkite (Memories Restaurant)

Bottom, left. Pat O'Brien (Memories Restaurant)

Bottom, right. Cousin Brucie, Paul "Wishbone" Brinegar, and Clint Eastwood at Palisades Park (Ed Hill)

Cronkite, William Shatner, Clint Eastwood, and former first lady Jacqueline Kennedy Onassis and her children, John-John and Caroline. Debbie Reynolds and Eddie Fisher announced their engagement at the Park. Buster Crabbe gave calisthenics lessons in the pool. Gus Lesnevich (the light heavyweight boxing champion of the world from 1941 to 1948) was a lifeguard there; when he wasn't working, he often put on sparring demonstrations. Once Kalid al Saud, the crown prince of Saudi Arabia, came to Palisades with his entire entourage to see the two-headed cow at the animal freak show. Another time, the King and Queen of Nepal visited the Park.

Palisades Amusement Park

•

Above, left. Worker paints the Cyclone roller coaster, 1967. (*The Record*)

Above, right. Worker readies the Jungleland ride, 1968. (*The Record*)

Left. Miniature golf course (Memories Restaurant)

They rode every ride, played every game, saw every sight—and wouldn't leave. The Park had to stay open late to accommodate them, and the concessionaires were livid.

Buddy Hackett, the renowned comedian, lived three blocks away from the amusement park in the Palisades section of Fort Lee. He later recalled, "The first time I went to the Park, I met two nice girls and had a great day. I was fourteen. . . . It was 1938. The last

time I was at the Park [in 1966], I took my wife and three children, I
met two nice girls . . . and my wife made me move to California!"

Many local residents avoided the roads near the Park between
April and September. Those who didn't usually were caught within a
traffic jam that stretched all the way to the George Washington
Bridge. Yet for all its success, the Park on the Palisades had physi-
cally not grown one acre since 1898, except for some thirteen acres
of Edgewater property acquired to accommodate additional parking.
Some in the area felt the Park had outgrown itself. Indeed, times had
changed at Palisades—and not all for the better.

Despite the Park's wave of popularity, an undercurrent of fear
and danger began to make itself known. Local residents had
protested that the growing crowds at the Park contained many out-
siders, most of whom usually brought trouble. "Riff raff"—the type
of people Irving Rosenthal hated most—were coming into his Park.
Palisades' rides were being vandalized, and cars in the parking lot
were broken into regularly. The maiden name of Mrs. Rosenthal,
Gladys Shelley, was a security code used whenever there was trouble in the Park—and it seemed to blare over the loudspeakers more
than ever before. On top of that, serious accidents were again

befalling the Park. In 1968, a girl was killed when a car broke loose from the revolving Disk Express. The next year a boy was killed when he became trapped underneath a boat in the shallow water-way of the Atomic Boat ride.

Rosenthal had hoped the Park would be carried on as a family business. Now in his seventies, he had suffered an undisclosed num-ber of heart attacks and had no children of his own, only a few nephews and nieces (including Anna Cook) who wanted no part of running the amusement park. Tired and ailing, he wanted out.

Above. Anna Cook (Cliffside Park
Free Public Library)

Right. View of the Park with Manhattan skyline in the background
(*The Record*)

Beginning in 1967, the towns of Cliffside Park and Fort Lee set
about to rid themselves of an amusement park that had become a
gaudy nuisance. That year the two towns got together to rezone the
property for high-rise development. Fort Lee had most of the input
regarding the rezoning because their town already had several high
rises dotting the Palisades. During the public hearings, no one raised
an objection—including Irving. Both towns rezoned the properties,
and developers from across the country focused their eyes on the
desirable land. Rosenthal began negotiations with prospective buyers.

By late 1969, rumors abounded that the amusement park was
going to close. The Park gone? What would they do with it? Who
would buy it? Though patrons continued to flood through the gates,
speculation only increased as Palisades entered a new decade.

Finally, on September 12, 1971, the rumors came true. That day,
the Park closed its gate for the last time; Rosenthal had sold Palisades to the Centex-Winston Corporation of Texas for $12.5 million.
Patrons were stunned as word spread; one New York elementary-
school class even sent a letter to President Richard Nixon, begging

Above, left. Aerial view of the Park showing nearby suburban homes (*The Record*/Dan Oliver)

Above, right. The crowded midways of the Park (Cliffside Park Free Public Library)

Below. Aerial view of the Park (Joan Mazzocchi-Lagasi and Pier Lagasi)

The Later Years, 1960–1971

•

him to intercede and keep the Park open. Many associated with the Park knew nothing of the sale until they read about it in the newspapers; this included Mickey Hughes, who by this time owned most of the rides. In an attempt to keep the Park open for one more season, Hughes negotiated with the Centex-Winston Corporation to lease the property for one year at a cost of $1 million. When word of the proposed deal reached the concessionaires, they were elated. Cheers rang out when Hughes drove into the Park in his Mercedes limousine. "They were cheering and clapping like I was a movie star," Hughes later recalled. "Everybody felt good about it."

Hughes obtained the necessary operating permit from Fort Lee, but Cliffside Park wouldn't be issuing their 1972 permits until January 7. On October 7, 1971, Hughes met with the executives of Centex to complete the deal. After some casual conversation, the men sat down to sign the lease.

Mickey said, "I'm going to give you a $100,000 certified check. I'm going to endorse it and give it to you. And I'm going to give you $900,000 that's going into escrow, in your bank or any bank, until I receive my permit on the seventh."

The vice president of Centex sat back in his chair, stared into Mickey's eyes, and said, "Mickey, when you sign this contract I want to have a million dollars to spend tomorrow morning."

Hughes glanced at his attorney, Jerry Pappas. Silence temporarily filled the room. Then Pappas said, "Let's go, Mickey," and the two men rose and started for the door. The Centex executive yelled, "Wait a minute! Wait a minute!" But Pappas and Hughes kept walking. They headed for the local tavern, where they discussed what had just occurred.

Later that same day, Hughes heard from Centex. "They dropped the price to $500,000," he said, "and before I went to bed I could have had the Park for free." By that time, though, Hughes felt uncomfortable with the deal. He had previously agreed to purchase whatever buildings and rides that Irving still had, provided the deal with Centex went through. Then the Park's bookkeeper claimed the pool's lockers were not included in the price. The final indignity was when the bookkeeper informed Hughes that, if the Park remained open for another season, Hughes would have to purchase the surrounding fence. The Park's fate was sealed.

Slowly, Palisades began to come down. Bits and pieces of the Park were sold to amusement areas around the country. The lights from the parking lot were carefully dismantled and wound up in the athletic field of nearby Ridgefield Park High School. The mayors of Cliffside Park, Fort Lee, and Edgewater met to discuss the feasibility

Aftermath of a Carousel—Round and Round It Went

There was no one item at Palisades Amusement Park that Irving Rosenthal treasured more than his carousel. Rosenthal loved the forty-three-year-old ride and wanted it to receive a good home. Finding one was not so easy, however.

The Straise Shows, one of the finest names in the carnival industry, wanted to buy the carousel. Rosenthal refused: he didn't want it to be with a carney.

NBC reporter Pia Lindstrum wanted to purchase one of the horses. Rosenthal refused: he didn't want to dismember it.

Jack Davis and John Crosby, who owned the Britannia Beach Hotel in Paradise Island, wanted the carousel for their hotel. Rosenthal refused: he felt the corrosive effect of the nearby saltwater would ruin it.

The government of Nigeria offered to buy it. Rosenthal refused: he didn't want it to be that far away.

Rosenthal offered to donate his beloved carousel to the Bergen County Parks Commission. The commission refused on the grounds it would be inappropriate for the county's parks. The Smithsonian also declined the offer, claiming it had no room.

Forest Park in Queens wanted to buy it to replace its carousel, which had burned down. But by the time Forest Park received its insurance check, Palisades had another buyer.

Bill Dredge came in from Lion Country Safari in Laguna Hills, California. Lion Country wanted to use the carousel as the center of a restaurant in a new safari park it planned to build in Monroe Township, New Jersey. Of all the prospective buyers, Dredge and his company proved the best.

Lion Country had planned to simply pack up the carousel and move it, but Rosenthal insisted it be done his way. He had Bert Whitworth, the Park's former head carpenter, pack the gingerbread, the mirrors, and the horse's legs, and he called in the people who wrapped the paintings for Sotheby Galleries to pack the horses.

In the meantime, Lion Country had encountered trouble getting the necessary zoning for the proposed park, and it asked Palisades to please store the carousel for a short while. A short while turned into a few years. The carousel, now in pieces, remained in trailers that were kept on Lemoine Avenue in Fort Lee until 1974, when the trailers had to be removed to make way for a shopping center.

Lion Country sold the carousel to King's Island in Cincinnati, which later sold it to its sister park, King's Dominion, located near Richmond. The carousel was finally sold to Canada's Wonderland in Maple, Ontario, where it remains today.

★ ★

of keeping the pool open for the use of local residents. But when they went to look it over, they discovered that most of the pipes and equipment had been pilfered or vandalized. They considered refurbishing, but that would be too costly.

In February 1972, the realization that this was indeed the end hit home. Joe McKee's world-famous Cyclone, purported to be the world's fastest roller coaster, was demolished and reduced to a pile

Above and left. Dismantling the rides (Cliffside Park Free Public Library and Bob Nesoff)

Below. The Cyclone coaster (P. J. Shelley/CPHS yearbook)

Palisades Amusement Park

•

Above. The Cyclone refuses to fall, February 4, 1972. (*The Record*/Gordon Corbett)

Right. A cloud of dust rises from the collapsing Cyclone. (*The Record*/Gordon Corbett)

Below. Debris of the Cyclone (*The Record*/Gordon Corbett)

Above, left. Firefighters battle the final blaze at the Park. (Memories Restaurant)

Above, right. Ruins of the Circus restaurant (*The Record*/Dan Oliver)

of lumber, nails, and memories. Bert Whitworth, the Park's former head carpenter, recalled years later, "When they started pulling down the roller coaster, it was like losing my right arm."

Eight days later, a five-alarm fire broke out in the bathhouses of the pool around 3:00 p.m., just as schoolchildren were returning home. Palisades Amusement Park gave the youngsters one last free exhibition they would never forget. The flames soared one hundred feet into the sky as firefighters from six towns tried to get the conflagration under control. Burning embers and pieces of smoldering wood spilled down the face of the cliffs, threatening the homes below.

The firefighters battled the blaze for three hours. By the time the last ember was extinguished, the bathhouses had been transformed into a pile of ashes and the Park's old Circus Restaurant had been left a blackened shell. The pool, which at one time had held 1½ million gallons of refreshing saltwater, now was filled with rubble, dirt, broken concrete, and charred wood.

Palisades had had its last disaster.

Despite its inconveniences, Palisades Amusement Park had

Left. High-rise condos replace the Park (Fred Morrone)

Above. Irving Rosenthal (Bob Nesoff)

been treasured by many residents, and its closing came as a blow. "It was chaos on Saturdays and Sundays with traffic and parking," recalled Ed Cavallo, who lived less than half a block away from the Park. "But when you're born in the area, the noise didn't bother you. I would rather have the Park. The high rises did nothing positive for the town."

Perhaps no one was more prophetic than Ed's grandfather, Alexander DeSiervo, who foresaw the future of Palisades long ago. "My grandfather, back in the thirties, predicted there would be tall buildings along the cliffs," Ed said. "Because New York was decaying, people would flee Manhattan and come here."

"The Park was part of me . . . I became part of the Park," Mickey Hughes reflected. "I was very depressed when it was finished."

At the time of closing, Cliffside Park was collecting an estimated $50,000 in taxes from Palisades. After the Park closed and the first two high-rises were occupied, the town was realizing approximately $3 million. Yet Cliffside Park Mayor Gerald Calabrese still reflects warmly on the Park: "Pleasant memories! Especially the school picnic days."

One former Fort Lee mayor said, "As a public official, I was glad to see it closed. There were a lot of complaints by residents. Yet personally I was saddened." Certainly, he was not the only one.

The Winston Towers, a condominium development with thirty-six hundred units, now stand on the thirty-eight-acre site of what many locals believe should be a public landmark. (Ironically, the towers surround the home of Anna Cook, who refused to sell to Centex-Winston.) No monument or marker has been erected to proclaim that the country's greatest amusement park once occupied this ground. Many believe there should be at least a street sign acknowledging the Park.

Irving Rosenthal probably would have agreed had he lived. Two years after the Park's closing, Rosenthal succumbed to a heart attack at the age of seventy-seven.

Epilogue

$\mathcal{T}$HE MYSTIQUE of Palisades Amusement Park has grown since the Park's closing. Some say ghosts still haunt the property on which Palisades stood. Many feel an odd, supernatural presence as they travel past the ground where thousands were entertained annually. What they are probably feeling is the reminiscences of happier days, of a time when people shared laughs and smiles on the midways of a great American fun center.

The value of Palisades' memorabilia is skyrocketing; posters, discount coupons, souvenir wallets, postcards, and banners are all fetching top dollar at flea markets and antique shops. In 1987 a new eatery opened in Fort Lee, Memories Restaurant, which featured fine food, a mesmerizing shark bar, an enormous larger-than-life mural depicting Cousin Brucie on stage at the Park, hundreds of Palisades photos on its walls, and an impressive display of Park memorabilia. Two years later, dozens of performers who received their start at Palisades—including Bobby Rydell, Freddy Cannon, Lesley Gore, and Little Anthony—performed at the Brendon Byrne Arena during a reunion festival hosted by Bruce Morrow. And in 1991, the Palisades Amusement Park Historical Society was formed. Newspaper clippings, magazine articles, hundreds of photos, and miles of film footage are being carefully preserved for future generations.

Perhaps it's best that Palisades Amusement Park closed when it did. The Park shut its gates long before video recorders, video games, or virtual-reality computers could steal away its patrons. It

★ ★

Update on Past Owners and Key Personnel

- The Bergen County Traction Company, the trolley line that first owned the Park, became the Public Service Bus Company. Later, deciding to make better use of the miles of power lines formerly used for the trolley, it became the Public Service Electric and Gas Company. It is now the state's largest utility and one of America's largest combined electric and gas companies, serving more than 5 ½ million residents throughout New Jersey.

- In April 1941, Joseph Schenck—"Honest Joe," as his Hollywood associates had nicknamed him—was convicted of tax evasion and served a three-year sentence at Danbury State Prison in Connecticut. He was later pardoned by President Harry S. Truman. He died in 1961 at the age of eighty-two.

- In 1955, as profits at MGM declined, the company's stockholders pressured Nick Schenck to resign. He died of a stroke in 1969 at his home in Miami Beach. He was eighty-seven years old.

- Anna Cook remained in her home, surrounded by the high-rise buildings of Centex, until she died in October 1992.

- John Rinaldi was hired by Fletch Creamer, a local construction company, after Palisades closed. Ironically, one of his first jobs was the demolition of the Park.

- Morgan "Mickey" Hughes continued to expand his successful ride-importing empire. Shortly after the closing of Palisades Amusement Park, Hughes purchased more than three hundred acres of property in Mechanicsburg, Pennsylvania, where he now runs a race track as well as Williams Grove Amusement Park.

★ ★

closed before any violent crime could have been accused of its downfall. It bowed out gracefully, leaving many fond memories as its legacy.

Many have defined spring as the time when daffodils and tulips bloom. Others defined spring as the time of year when Palisades Amusement Park opened its gates for another season of laughs, thrills, and happiness. To these people, springtime has never quite been the same.

Appendix A: Plot Plan (1953)

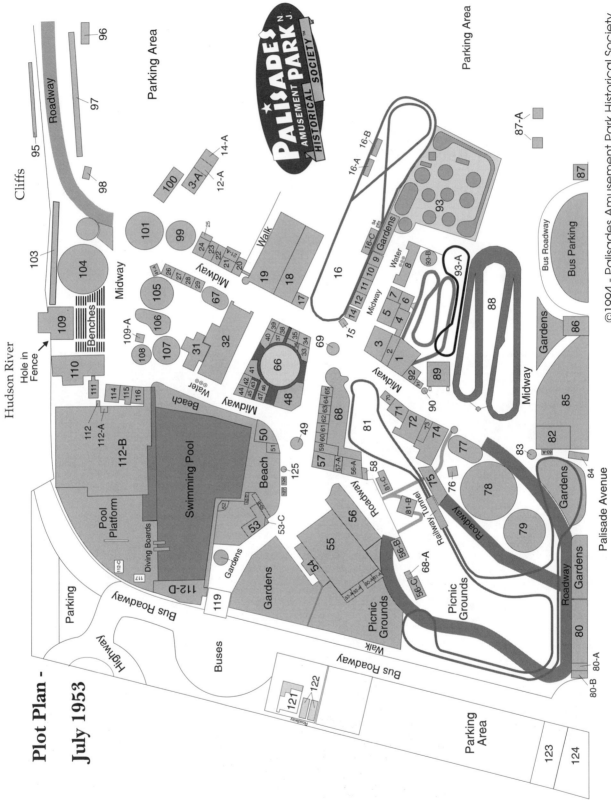

Plot Plan -
July 1953

Hudson River

Cliffs

Parking Area

Parking Area

Parking Area

©1994 - Palisades Amusement Park Historical Society

1. Auto Speedway
2. Clock Wheel
3. Combination
3A. C & D Storeroom
4. Electrical Shop
5. Pokerino
6. Auto Speedway shop
7. Ham Wheel
8. Toilets
9. Cigar Stand
10. Luncheonette
11. Potato Chip
12. Grocery Wheel
12A. Corcoran Storeroom
14. Toy Wheel
14A. Lipner Storeroom
15. Candy Floss
16. Cyclone
16A. Cyclone Motor House
16B. Cyclone Storeroom
16C. Cyclone Shop
17. Doll Wheel
18. Bingo
19. Arcade
20. Bird Wheel
21. Barrel Game
21A. Lamp Storeroom
22. Doll Wheel
23. Gift Wheel
24. Scale Wheel
25. Transformer
26. Balloon Game
27. Cat Game
28. Birch Beer
29. Roast Beef
31. Pin Ball
32. Auto Skooter
33. String Game
34. Carousel Custard Stand
35. Dog Wheel
36. Custard Storeroom
37. Transformer
38. Cigarette Wheel
39. Big Color Wheel
40. Milk Bottle Game
41. Hamburger Stand
41A. High Striker
42. Greyhound Race
43. Waffle Storeroom
44. Waffle Stand
45. Grocery Wheel
46. Souvenir Storeroom
47. Cigarette Wheel

48. Candyland
49. Mouse Game
50. Pool Frankfurter Stand
51. Pool Custard Stand
52. Casino Band Stand
53. Casino
53A. Casino Storeroom
53B. Casino Icebox
53C. Casino Snack Bar
53D. Pool Snack Stand
54. Toilets
55. Fun House
55A. Fun House Storeroom
56. Administration Building
56A. Storeroom
56B. Garage
56C. Plumbing Shop
57. Shooting Gallery
57A. Shooting Gallery Storeroom
58. Transformer
59. Photo Gallery
60. Doll Wheel
61. Candy Wheel
61A. Fletch Storeroom
62. Ham & Bacon Wheel
63. Penny Pitch
64. Radio Wheel
65. Souvenir Stand
66. Carousel
67. Hay-Day
68. Tunnel of Love
68A. Aluminum Shed
69. Information Booth
70. Palmistry
71. Roast Beef
72. Shooting Gallery
73. Pan Game
74. Fascination
75. Carpenter Shop
76. Transformer
77. Whip
78. Flying Scooter
79. Lion Drome
80. Storage Building (Ferguson)
80A. Garage
80B. Ferguson's Office
81. Miniature Railway
81A. Railway Tunnel
81B. House
81C. Norge House
82. Sun Burst Stand
83. Octagon Stand
83A. Octagon Storeroom

84. Transformer (P.S.)
85. Golf Course
86. Palisade Gate
87. Auto Gate House
87A. Auto Ticket Booths
88. Water Skooter
89. Cuddle Up
90. Guess Your Age
90A. Goldberg Storeroom
91. Potato Chip
92. Speedway Custard
93. Kiddieland
93A. Palisade Giant
93B. Rodeo
94. Transformer
95. Surf Bathing Sign
96. Searchlights
97. Palisades Amusement Park
     Sign
98. Old Bobsled Motor House
99. Tilt a Whirl
100. Packard Storeroom
101. Hurricane
103. Moving Sign
104. Love Bugs
105. Magnet Drome
106. Boomerang
107. Jet Plane
108. Caterpillar
109. Free Act Stage
109A. Free Act Searchlight Building
110. Restaurant
111. Ferris Wheel
112. Transformer
112A. Sprinkler System Room
112B. Bathhouse
112C. Laundry
112D. Filter Room
114. Midget Movies
115. Potato Chip
116. Frankfurter Stand
117. Pool Platform Restaurant
      Stand
119. Hudson Gate
121. House
122. Greenhouses
123. Three-Family House
124. Workshop (1002 Palisade
      Ave.)
125. Scale
126. Handwriting Stand
127. Hat Stand
128. Scale

Appendix B: The Rides

Below is a partial listing of various rides that Palisades Amusement Park housed over the decades.

Aero-Swing
Antique Cars
Apollo 14
Arabian Nights Tunnel of Love
Atomic Boats
Auto Skooter
Auto Speedway
Automobile Race
Batman Slide
The Bee Hive
Big Scenic Coaster
Bombardment
Boomerang Ride
The Bowl
Bubble Bounce
Carousel (PTC model #84)
Casper's Ghostland
Caterpillar
Chair-o-Plane
Channel Boat
Chariot Race
Children's Playground
Children's Village
Chinatown
Circle Swing
Cleopatra's Barge
Cockeyed Circus (fun house)

Comet
Crazy Crystals Glass House
Crazy Dazy
Crazy House
Crystal Maze
Cuddle Up
Cyclone
Deep Dip Thriller Coaster
Devil's Jig Saw
Dodgem
Double Loop-a-Plane
1865 Trains
Electric Go Carts
Electric Wagon Bump Ride
Ferris Wheel
Figure 8 Toboggan Coaster
Flying Airships
Flying Bobs
The Flying Cages
Flying Coaster
Flying Saucer
Flying Scooter
Fun House
Fun Slide
Giant Coaster
Giant Slide
Giant Wheel

Green's Pony Tract
Greyhound Races
Gyroplane
Hay-Dey
Helicopter
Hurricane Rotor
Ice Skating Rink
Jaguarbahn
Jet Plane
Jitterbug Ride
Katzenjammer House
Kiddieland (35 rides)
Lake Placid Bob Sled Coaster
Lindy Loop
Loop-de-Loop
Looper
Loop-o-Plane
MacArthur Bomber
Merry-Go-Round
Merry Mixer
Meteor
The Mill on the Floss
Miniature Railroad
Monorail
Monster
Motorboat Ride
Motor Parkway
The Octopus
Oktoberfest
The Old Mill
Over the Falls
Palisades Riding Academy
Parachute Ride
The Pony Tract
Racer
The Racing Toboggan
Revel
Rise and Fall of New York City
The Rocket
Rock-o-Plane
Rodeo
Roll-o-Plane
Round Up
Schiff Kiddie Coaster
The Scooter
Scrambler
Scup Swings
Shooting the Rapids
Shoot-the-Chute
Showboat Fun House
Skydiver
Sky Fighter
Sky Ride
Skyrocket Coaster
Sleighride Coaster

Small Scenic Railway
The Snapper
Space Rocket
Space Wheel
Spider House
Strato Ship
The Streamlines
Super Himalaya
Swan Ride
The Thing
Third Degree
Through the Dardanelles
Tilt-a-Whirl
Tip Top
Tower Slide
Trabant
Traver Cyclone Coaster
Tub Race
Tumble Bug
The Tunnel of Love
Turnpike Ride
20,000 Leagues under the Sea
The Twister
U Drive 'Em Boats
Venice
Virginia Reel
Water Ride
Water Scooter
Wendy's Cups 'n' Saucers
The Whip
Whirligig
Whirlpool
Wild Mouse Coaster
Witching Waves

**Examples of
Mickey Hughes's rides:**

Airborne
Bayern Curve
Calypso Ride
Cortina Bob
Disk Express
Flight to Mars
French Himalaya
German Carousel
German Scooter Ride
Giant Riesenrad Wheel
Globe of Death
Go Carts
Grand Prix
Himalaya
Hoffrahaus
Hootenany (Calypso)
Hot Rod Cars
Jet Star Coaster

Jungleland
Love Bugs
Magnadrome
Matterhorn
Music Express
Polyp
Rotor (Magnadrome)
Rotor Jet
Satellite Jet

Sprung Schanze
Super Himalaya
Swiss Bobs (Bayern Curve)
Trip to the Moon
25th Century Monorail
Von Roll Cable Sky Ride
Wildcat Coaster
Zugspitz

Palisades Amusement Park

•

Appendix C: The Attractions

Nearly everything housed within the gates of Palisades Amusement Park was considered an attraction. The following list was compiled from published sources and it is only a partial collection of the many features of the Park.

Attractions

Aerodome
Banjo Palace
Children's Playground
Creation: The World of the Unborn
Dance Pavilion
Dr. Schultz's Infant Incubators
Entertainment Hall
The Farm
Fish Pond
Handball Courts
Hippodrome
James Bond's Astin Martin car
Lover's Lane
Lustron House
McAndrew's Lamp Stamp
Midget Movies
Millican's Hindu Theatre
Miniature Golf Course
Mitchell's Snake Show
Moving World
Norge House
Palisades Amusement Park
    Observatory

Picnic Tables
Punch and Judy Show
Roller Skating Rink
Saltwater Swimming Pool
Skating Lake
Swiss Chalet Museum
Tea Gardens
Williard's Temple of Music
WPAP Radio Station
Zoological Gardens

Games

Apple Game
Balloon Game
Barrel Game
The Basketball Game
Bingo
The Cane Board
Cat Game
Days of '49
Disk Stein Board
Fascination Game
Goldfish Game
Greyhound Race

High Striker
Knife Board
Milk Bottle Game
Mouse Game
Pan Game
Penny Arcade
Penny Pitch
Pinball
Pokerino
Skee Ball
Skillo
String Game

Wheels

Big Color Wheel
Bird Wheel
Candy Wheel
Cigarette Wheel
Clock Wheel
Dog Wheel
Doll Wheel
Gift Wheel
Grocery Wheel
Ham and Bacon Wheel
Ham Wheel
Radio Wheel
Scale Wheel
Toy Wheel

Stands

Cigar Stand
007 Shooting Gallery

Green Beret Shooting Gallery
Guess Your Age
Guess Your Weight
Handwriting Stand
Hat Stand
Information Booth
Octagon Stand
Palmistry
Photo Gallery
Shooting Gallery
Soothsayer Booth
Souvenir Stand

Food Stands

Belgian Waffles
Candyland
Casino restaurant
Circus Restaurant
Cotton Candy (Candy floss)
Frankfurter
French Fries (Potato Chips)
Frozen Custard
Genuine Rhode Island Clam
   Bake
Harry's Hamburgers
Lemonade
Mampe, The Candy Man
Mrs. Noffka's Lunch Room
Pat and Gary's
Paul's Clam Chowder
Refreshment Pavilion
Roast Beef

Appendix D: The Entertainment

Destroyed, missing, and incomplete records yield only a small percentage of the names of those headliners that played on the cliffs of the Palisades. But those that are known are listed below in rough chronological order.

May Ward
The Four Sinclairs
Anita Bondi
Charles Strickland Orchestra
N.T.G. and His Radio Pals
The Great Sir Joseph Ginzberg
Tommy Christian and His
  Orches-tra
Benny Goodman's Big Band
Ted Steele and His Big Band
Cab Calloway and His Band
Les Brown and His Orchestra
Don Redman and His Orchestra
Bunny Berigan and Orchestra
Buddy Ebsen
Bob Chester and Orchestra
Louis Prima and His Orchestra
The Bailey Sisters
Uncle Don
Enoch Light and His Orchestra
Bob Tucker and His Orchestra
Joe Venuti
Kay Starr
The "Swing Shift Frolics"

Ted Flo Rito and His Orchestra
George Paxton and His Orchestra
Shep Fields Orchestra
Art Mooney and His Orchestra
Fran Warren
Nat Brusiloff and His Orchestra
Russ Irwin and His Orchestra
Buddy Breese
Ray Anthony and His Orchestra
Dick Merrick
Tommy Ryan and His Orchestra
Sam Donahue and His Orchestra
Les Elgart and His Orchestra
Henry Busse and His Orchestra
Johnny Messner and His Orchestra
George Towne and His Orchestra
Harry James
The Dorsey Brothers
Xavier Cugat
Cousin Bruce Morrow
Fabian
Chubby Checker
Bobby Lewis
Chuck Jackson

The Shirelles
The Regents
Frank Gari
The Echoes
The Visconts
Jo Ann Campbell
Cathy Jean
The Roommates
The Rays
The Bobettes
Bob Crewe
Nino and the Ebbtides
The Jive Five
The Mello Kings
Ronnie Savoy
Timi Yuro
The Earls
The Mystics
Donnie and the Dreamers
The Chiffons
The Orlons
The Crystals

Leslie Gore
The Jackson Five
Hal Jackson
Dagmar and Bernadette Castro
Tony Bennett
Vic Damone
The Four Seasons
Bill Haley and the Comets
Bobby Rydell
Dion
Jackie Wilson
Neil Sedaka
Tony Orlando
Frankie Avalon
Little Anthony
The Tokens
Lenny CoCo and the Chimes
Freddy Cannon
Diana Ross and the Supremes
The Young Rascals
The Loving Spoonful
The Fifth Dimension

Appendix E: Attendance

Record Attendance Figures (As Reported by Palisades Amusement Park)

May 30, 1908
  3,000—opening day

May 28, 1908
  30,000—opening weekend

May 30, 1909
  40,000—largest single-day gate to date

August 7, 1915
  27,000

August 10, 1923
  61,235—Saturday
  67,800—Sunday

August 31, 1923
  200,000—weekly

July 4, 1924
  57,234

April 17, 1925
  1,500,000—yearly

July 26, 1929 (20-year statistics compiled by *The Palisadian*)
  Park season averages:
  98 weekdays at 10,000 each = 980,000 x 20 years = 19,600,000
  40 weekends at 25,000 each = 1,000,000 x 20 years = 20,000,000
  *3 holidays at 25,000 each = 75,000 x 20 years = 1,500,000

*4th of July, Decoration Day (Memorial Day), Labor Day

Total yearly average 2,055,000
Total 20 year attendance 41,100,000

June 5, 1936
    10,000—daily

July 10, 1936
    150,000—largest single-day gate to date (July 4th)
    100,000—July 5

March 31, 1949
    6,500,000—1948 annual

April 5, 1953
    15,000—opening day

July 11, 1954
    150,000—largest single-day gate to date

June 1, 1959
    260,000—Memorial Day weekend
    126,000—May 31st

Summer 1964
    4,000,000—yearly

1969
    10,000,000—yearly

Sunday, May 1970
    213,000

1971
    7,200,000—yearly

January 24, 1971
    300,000,000—total park history since 1897

December 20, 1992
    Palisades Amusement Park Historical Society estimates average
    annual attendance at 6,000,000

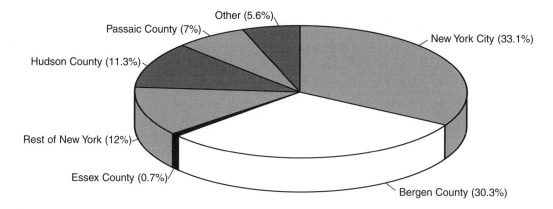

Breakdown by area is based upon research statistics compiled by the Palisades Amusement Park Historic
Society. It is based on information published throughout the lifetime of the Park and not on any one particular date.

Palisades Amusement Park
•

Appendix F: Competition

Palisades had competition throughout its lifetime. From the Boardwalks of South Jersey to the glitter of Coney Island, the Park always had to stay on the cutting edge to compete.

Astroland, Coney Island, N.Y.*
Bergen Point, Bayonne, N.J.
Bertrand Park, Hopatcong, N.J.
Clementon Park, Clementon, N.J.
Columbia Park, North Bergen, N.J.
Columbia Park, Union City, N.J.
Dreamland Park, Coney Island, N.Y.
Fairyland Park, Paterson, N.J.
Fort George, New York, N.Y.
Freedomland, New York, N.Y.
Golden City Park Arena, Canarsie, Brooklyn, N.Y.
Hunt's Pier, Wildwood, N.J.
Luna Park, Coney Island, N.Y.
Midland Beach, Staten Island, N.Y.
Olympic Park, Irvington, N.J.
Olympic Park, Maplewood, N.J.
Olympic Park, Newark, N.J.
Paradise Park, Fort George, New York, N.Y.
Playland, Rockaway, Queens, N.Y.
Playland, Rye, N.Y. *
Rockaway Beach, Long Island, N.Y.
Sea Lion Park, Brooklyn, N.Y.
Starlight Park, Bronx, N.Y.
Steeplechase Park, Coney Island, N.Y.
Wild West City, New Jersey
Woodland Park, Trenton, N.J.
World's Fair, Flushing Meadows, N.Y. (1939, 1964)

Many have reflected how there has never been another place like Palisades Amusement Park. Although this is a sad truth, there are many fine amusement parks still entertaining crowds today. Some share similarities to Palisades.

- Big Surf in Arizona boasts the largest man-made pool, including surf.
- Rye Playland in Rye, New York, has preserved much of its historic ele-

* still in existence

ments. It features a Kiddieland with twenty rides specifically designed for the children and an outdoor stage with concerts throughout the summer.

- Tucked away in the woods of Mechanicsburg, Pennsylvania, is Williams Grove Amusement Park. A wonderful place to bring the family, this park features rides and attractions for all ages including a miniature golf course and beautiful picnic groves.
- Dorney Park was a former trolley park that survived the decades. It features a wave pool, a classic wooden coaster named "Hercules," picnic groves, and live shows.
- Of all the amusement parks in the world today, the one park that shares the most similarities to Palisades Amusement Park is Kennywood in West Mifflin, Pennsylvania. Like Palisades, Kennywood sits atop a high bluff and overlooks a river. It began as a trolley park in 1898 (the same year as Palisades) and it is very close in size. It has even built itself a reputation for having the nation's best amusement park french fries.

Bibliography

Adams, Judith A., and Edwin J. Perkins. *The American Amusement Park Industry: A History of Technology and Thrills*. Boston: Twayne, 1991.

Barris, Chuck. *Game Show King: A Confession*. New York: Carroll and Graf, 1993.

Cartmell, Robert. *The Incredible Scream Machine: A History of the Roller Coaster*. Bowling Green, Ohio: Bowling Green University Press, 1988.

Federal Writers' Project. *Bergen County Panorama*. [Elizabeth: Printed by Colby and McGowan], 1941.

Griffin, Al. *Step Right Up Folks*. Chicago: Henry Regnery, 1974.

Kyriazi, Gary. *The Great American Amusement Parks: A Pictorial History*. Secaucus, N.J.: Castle Books, 1976.

McCullough, Edo. *World's Fair Midways: An Affectionate Account of American Amusement Areas from the from the Crystal Palace to the Crystal Ball*. 1966. Reprint. Manchester, N.H.: Ayer, 1976.

Mangels, William F. *The Outdoor Amusement Industry*. New York: Vantage Press, 1952.

Morrow, Bruce, and Laura Baudo. *Cousin Brucie: My Life in Rock 'n' roll Radio*. New York: Beech Tree Books, 1987.

Siegel, Alan A. *Smile: A Picture History of Olympic Park, 1887-1965*. Irvington, N.J.: Irvington Historical Society, 1983.

Index

About the Author

Vince Gargiulo is the founder and executive director of the Palisades Amusement Park Historical Society. He was born and raised in Cliffside Park, a short distance from the Park. Mr. Gargiulo has been involved in many areas of entertainment, and currently owns Desktop Creations, a graphic arts firm.